Contents

Introduction

iii

HOOKED --on GOD!

VINCENT GUERRA

WARNER PRESS
ANDERSON INDIANA

Publisher's Foreword

"One of the best avenues, I feel, for promoting understanding and insight into exactly what it is like to be a victim of drug addiction is first person testimonies like Mr. Guerra's."

So wrote the noted Art Linkletter in introducing Vince Guerra's first book, *Turning Point,* which told the story of Vince's years as a drug addict and how the "turning point" came in his own life.

As a Christian minister, Vince Guerra now devotes his life to the rescue and rehabilitation of other young men and women, who like himself, have become "hooked" on various kinds of drugs. Having experienced rescue himself, and knowing first-hand what this crisis means in the life of a young person, his devotion to Christ and his skill in counseling have become the turning point for others.

This book continues Vince's story, but now it is the rescue of others that becomes central. Vince is still "hooked" but on God now and he knows the "answer," the way of escape from being hooked on drugs.

So this is the story of a crusade against the slavery of drug abuse. Vince Guerra tells how it is in Miami's flower culture, coffee houses, rap sessions, communes, and jails —anywhere and everywhere the cry for help comes.

Success stories are here, how a young boy turns from dope to Jesus Christ and reenters the world of reality.

Some of the other kind are here as well—how a young woman addict momentarily turns away from drugs, but succumbs to the powerful magnetism of drug-induced fantasia and eventually dies a horrible death.

This book centers around a "half-way house" type of ministry, and both the heartbreak and the heartwarming aspects of the work are here. This is a chronicle of Christianity in action in the midst of the drug scene. It points to a viable alternative to being "hooked" on drugs— being Hooked—On God!

1

Life in a New Vein

It was half-past twelve when I arrived home that summer night. Dog-tired, I fixed myself a snack in the kitchen, then went to bed. My wife, Ruth, was already asleep, and it didn't take me any time at all to ease my weary frame onto the bed. In moments I was sleeping soundly.

Sometime later, a tapping sound broke into my unconscious state. I thought, it must be raining! But shaking the sleep from my mind, I realized the taps came in threes. Tap. Tap. Tap. I jumped up, pulled on my trousers, and went to the window. As I pushed back the shade, I saw my partner, Glenn Bondurant. Glenn was grinning as he said, "Hey, man, you've had your two hours of sleep for the day, it's time to rise and shine now!"

I tried to focus my eyes on the clock, but couldn't decide whether it said three or four A.M. I turned back to my nightowl friend and growled, "What in the world are you doing? Are you crazy or something?"

He cheerfully replied, "Open the door. I have something for you!" I thought to myself, If this guy is playing games, I'm going to punch him! But I went to the door, opened it, and in walked Glenn followed by a skinny, weak-looking girl! I looked wide-eyed from him to her, and finally invited them to sit down.

Glenn told me the girl's name was Nancy. It was apparent that she needed help. Glenn said she had gone to a mental hygiene clinic where she had received Glenn's name and phone number. While she was having a bad experience tripping on LSD, Nancy had fished in her purse, found Glenn's number, and called him. And he, not knowing what else to do, had brought her to my home. He asked me to keep Nancy with Ruth and me until we got our halfway house.

Nancy had her pinched, pale face turned downward toward the floor. To my questions, she related that during her bad trip she had thought of committing suicide. She said she didn't know what else to do. When she looked up, I saw her undernourished face, her brown eyes, sad and appealing, and I said, "Sure, you can stay here, Nancy."

Our house had a small room off to the side of the carport, and I told Nancy she could occupy this room as long as she liked. When she heard me say this, she seemed to perk up, not unlike a stray dog that hears a kind word. Nancy looked up at me and smiled slightly.

I asked Glenn to wait a moment while I went into my bedroom to ask Ruth if it was all right to allow Nancy to stay at our house. Upon hearing Nancy's story, Ruth said, "Of course she can stay. It'll be good to have another girl around here, someone I can talk with." So I introduced Ruth to Nancy, then Ruth took her to the small room in which she was to stay. There Ruth searched Nancy and her belongings to see if drugs were hidden on her. Nancy insisted rightfully that she was clean, that she had no drugs.

Before leaving, Glenn thanked me for taking Nancy in. I laughed and reminded him there had been little alternative. His brow furrowed in deep thought as he said, "Someday we'll get that halfway house. Then we won't be going through these hassles anymore." We shook hands and he left.

After Ruth went through Nancy's belongings, I called them back to the living room to ask Nancy some questions. She said she was almost twenty years old, had been on drugs approximately two years, was using pot (marijuana), LSD, and other hallucinogenics. She said she had flashbacks every day, but denied ever using heroin. Nancy admitted having tried to use heroin, but became too frightened to use it each time she tried.

I asked her how she got money to buy drugs. She replied, "Most of the time I get drugs for nothing. I have a relative who is a pusher. He sells pot. I got mine from him." She denied having been a prostitute, adding that she usually worked as a waitress in restaurants. Nancy was not ignorant. She was quite articulate once she began talking and informed me she had completed one year at a university.

"Why did you start to use drugs?" I asked.

"It started with liquor parties with my college girl friends," she admitted. "At one of the parties a friend encouraged me to smoke pot. I tried it, and enjoyed it." She told how that start led her down a path toward complete addiction and horror.

Suddenly noticing the sun peeping over the western horizon, I looked at Nancy's reddened eyes and knew she needed rest. I told her to sleep late if she wished. Then I said, "Before you go to bed, Nancy, let's bow our heads and pray for God's guidance." Then she went to her room. Soon I was sound asleep—for the second time that night.

Waking at 9:30, I smelled the coffee Ruth had already prepared. After readying myself for breakfast, I knocked on Nancy's door to see if she wished to eat with us. She said she didn't want anything. For some reason she was timid, seemingly afraid to come out of her room. She sounded fidgety and confused. Finally I offered her a cup of coffee and she came out and sat down at the table with us.

Like a rabbit without protective cover, Nancy was withdrawn and seemed uncomfortable sitting at the table with Ruth and me. Ruth tried to break the ice by asking Nancy where her home was. She replied that she came from a small town near Chicago, that she had been in Florida not quite a year.

When I asked about her parents, Nancy glared at me and stated flatly, "I don't want to go into that." I dropped the question, but later learned Nancy had both father and mother.

While Nancy sipped her coffee, she pulled a cigarette from her purse. Ruth glanced at me, since we both dislike having anyone smoke in our home. But I said nothing to Nancy, not wanting to upset her any more than was necessary. She was really uptight.

Before Ruth and I finished breakfast, Nancy suddenly announced, "I've got to go!" I asked why, and she said, "I just have to get out! I have to get away!" Asked where she intended to go, she replied, "Just for a ride."

I stood up and said, "Look, Nancy, you can stay here, but don't think you can come and go as you please. This is not a flophouse. It's our home."

She looked up at me, smiled slightly, and said, "I realize that. But I just have to get out. I feel as though the walls are closing in on me."

I said, "All right. But remember one thing: there are going to be rules laid down to you if you stay here. If you don't like the rules, then you'll have to go." She said that was okay, but still wanted to get out for five or ten minutes. I agreed, and she jumped into her '64 Chevrolet and drove off.

Ruth linked her arm through mine and said, "Vince, I don't like it. This girl seems to need professional treatment."

I replied, "Perhaps you're right. We'll take her Monday to Henderson Clinic for psychiatric evaluation." I sat on the porch waiting for Nancy to come back. In about ten minutes her car pulled up in front of the house. I leaned back to relax in my chair.

Nancy walked up to me and said, "Thanks for letting me go. I just had to get away." I asked her if she had taken any drugs. "No," she replied, "I wouldn't do that to you people since you were kind enough to take me in." I asked her again if she had any marijuana in her possession. She said, "No, but if you look on the floor in the back seat of my car, you'll see a mess of seeds."

Immediately I checked her car, found the seeds, and scraped them up. I swept out her car and dumped the seeds in the garbage pail, knowing Nancy would have been arrested for illegal possession of marijuana if an officer had stopped her and searched the car.

A week passed and Nancy began to make progress. Responsive to the Christian love Ruth and I tried to share with her she developed a great liking for our year-old son, Jackie. Often, I returned to the house for dinner to find Nancy and Jackie playing on the floor. Recalling the frail-looking girl she had been, I had thought she might break in two if she bent the wrong way. Now she was gaining weight and health was returning. Her skin tone began to look alive as it lost sallowness.

But one night she told me she was having flashbacks, causing her to "trip" the whole night through. This kept her from sleeping properly. I hardly knew what to advise her about the flashbacks. Since I am not a doctor, I had no medicine to prescribe. But I did know that Jesus Christ, our Lord and Savior, would help her if only Nancy would open her heart to him.

Thursday nights for me center around our drug rehabilitation meetings held at the House of Ichthus in Fort Lauderdale. It's a clean, little coffeehouse where on weekends young people go to listen to folk music and share some of their problems with our staff. On Thursday nights we have closed sessions for those who have been on drugs, or those who are on drugs and want to get off. I felt that Nancy could find help through attending these meetings.

Riding with me as I drove to Fort Lauderdale the next Thursday night, Nancy at last told me why she and her brother left home. She said her brother, Jay, was on marijuana and she hoped to get help for him too. Reluctantly, but clearly, she described her homelife. Her mother and father had been divorced, then her mother remarried. The stepfather was disliked by all the children. When she became old enough, Nancy left home.

She also told me about the night she was walking home from work when a fellow she slightly knew stopped his car to ask if she wanted a ride. She told him no and continued to walk. But the man got out, dragged her into his car, took her out into a lonely woods, and criminally asaulted her. This affected her emotionally.

She confessed she often wanted to run away and kill herself. As we pulled into a parking space at the House of Ichthus, I said to Nancy, "God can help you through these times of depression, and give you a new life. I want you to know that he does care what happens to you."

She replied, "I find that a little difficult to believe, Vince. But since I've seen what he has done in your life, I know that if I open up to him, he can do the same in mine." Entering the coffeehouse, we saw several youth who have had experiences similar to Nancy's. Some of them reminded me of my own past involvement with drugs, an entanglement from which Christ had rescued me by his grace and power.

Glenn Bondurant saw us and came immediately to talk with Nancy. He expressed amazement to see that Nancy had gained weight. She laughed and said, "With all that good Italian food, what else can I do but put on weight?"

The encounter session that night was not long, but Nancy's patience soon wore thin. She had on her face the same look I'd noticed the night she had come to our house. I tapped her on the arm and said, "Come on, let's get out of here." Then I signaled Glenn to tell him Nancy wasn't feeling well, that I felt she should get out of the coffeehouse. He nodded his approval and we left.

Soon we were driving smoothly along I-95 talking about Nancy's childhood and church activities. It seems she had attended a Baptist church as a young girl and had been active in Sunday school. When I asked if her mother was a Christian, Nancy replied that to the best of her knowledge her mother had accepted Christ in a church service. Asked if she had made a commitment to Christ, Nancy replied, "Yes, I accepted Christ when I was a young girl, but never really followed it through."

I asked her why she had left the church. She said she left it when she was fourteen or fifteen, because there was so much hypocrisy in the church. She saw people who professed to be Christians, but did not live like it outside the worship services. Even in her own family, she felt she saw hypocrisy in her mother, who smoked and drank.

Nancy said she felt a Christian's life should be different from those who made no profession, and that a Christian life was one of holiness and service to God, whether as missionary, minister, office worker, high school or college student, serving God without conforming to the ways of the world. She said she left the church because of persons who said they loved Christ but lived lives of degradation and wickedness, but she could see through their lies.

I asked her if she felt it was wrong to use drugs and abuse her body. Nancy replied that she definitely felt wrong in doing such things, that she had sinned against Christ. As we drove, I asked, "Nancy, do you really think you gave yourself to Jesus Christ and accepted him as your Savior and Lord when you were younger?" She affirmed that she had done so.

Then I said, "Since you have sinned against Christ and lived the life you have, shouldn't you confess your sins to him and ask him for forgiveness?" She looked at me with a confused expression on her face, so I said, "You ought to rededicate your life to Christ." I asked her to bow her head and ask Jesus Christ to forgive her past sins and restore her relationship with him. I quoted 1 John 1:9, from Good News for Modern Man: "But if we confess our sins to God, we can trust him, for he does what is right—he will forgive us our sins and make us clean from all our wrongdoing." After repeating this verse, I said to Nancy, "Well, how about it? Why not dedicate your life to him and become a Christian?"

Nancy said quietly, "I think I'd like that, Vince." By that time we had arrived back at my house, so there in the carport Nancy and I bowed our heads in prayer. Slowly she repeated the prayer I worded. It was simple and Nancy's voice reflected how deeply she felt its meaning. She prayed, "Dear God, I have sinned against your Son Jesus Christ. I am truly sorry for those sins, and I am asking your Son to forgive me for all my wrongdoings. By faith I recommit my life to him. Amen."

Just those few—yet meaningful words, and Nancy knew she was truly God's child. And yet her battles were not over. That night as she prepared for bed, I heard her scream my name. Hurrying to her room I heard her gasp, "I think I'm going to have a flashback." She was horrified to think those drug-induced nightmares might recur. I called Ruth and asked her to hold one of Nancy's hands while I held the other. Together we prayed for release and victory over the drug demon. I prayed more earnestly than ever before, and soon Nancy said she felt she would be all right. That night she had restful sleep.

The change in Nancy was marked. When she first came to us she couldn't decide even simple matters. She would ask Ruth or me if she should drink coffee. Often she forgot our names, calling me Jackie—Jackie Vince —and Ruth something else. She seemed completely disoriented at times.

Often, Nancy left water running in the bathroom, or forgot to flush the toilet. Ruth often wondered if it was through neglect or damage resulting from Nancy's use of LSD. When I brought these matters to her attention, Nancy did not recall doing them. We constantly had to follow her to turn off lights, shut off the water, turn off the burners on the stove. We were especially concerned about little Jackie at the time, because he was most inquisitive about water running in the bathroom. Sometimes he rubbed against the hot stove and burned himself. Fortunately, his injuries were not serious—although we always wondered what was coming next.

Nancy was always quick to apologize. When she said, "I'm sorry," she meant it. And we knew it. During the two-and-one-half months she stayed with us Nancy became adept at doing household chores. Only one matter bothered us: Nancy continued to smoke. We often discussed with her what this did to her health. I approached it from the standpoint of ethics. I reminded her of Paul's admonition in 2 Corinthians 6:16, which reads, "For ye are the temple of the living God; as God has said, 'I will dwell in them, and walk in them; and I will be their God, and they shall be my people.'"

I carefully explained to Nancy that by smoking and inhaling the nicotine—another form of narcotic—she defiled God's temple. And if persons who are not Christians see us doing such things, could they not wonder if we are different from themselves? Nancy began to think seriously about her smoking, then one evening confided to me, "Vince, I think I'm going to stop smoking, because God has laid it upon my heart."

Nancy's battle to give up cigarettes began—a battle she won—although it took about two months to overcome her smoking hangup. She left our home only after we found her a home where she would have more privacy, and where she could effectively witness for the Lord.

2

A Groovy Experience

The night Nancy left our home, Ruth and I sat talking in our living room. The shrill jangle of the telephone interrupted our conversation. The caller. was the pastor of a congregation in the Hollywood, Florida, community. His words were to the point: "Vince, would you go to see a young girl named Mary? She needs help desperately."

I asked what her problem was and he replied that she was on drugs. He gave me Mary's name and address and that night, after a speaking engagement, I went to Fort Lauderdale to see Glenn and Barbara Bondurant, fellow staffers in our Turning Point ministry.

"Glenn, old buddy," I began, "I'd like for Barbara to go with me to visit a girl on drugs." We have a standing policy that a male counselor does not counsel with a female unless another female counselor is with him. On rare occasions, of course, only another male counselor is available, but discretion and care are exercised in each counseling situation.

Barbara and Glenn agreed that she should go with me to see Mary, and we also felt this would be a good opportunity for Nancy to go along to share what Christ had done for her. Soon Barbara, Nancy, and I reached

Mary's house. Responding to the doorbell, Mary's mother greeted us and said Mary was sleeping. When we identified ourselves as being with Turning Point ministry, the woman cordially invited us in. When we were seated Mary's mother said she would bring her to us and went to wake her.

A few minutes later the woman returned with Mary, a lovely young girl with long, blonde hair and startlingly blue eyes. I stood and introduced myself and the two women with me. Mary was dubious, thinking we were police. "Mary," I said, "there's nothing to be afraid of. We are here because we want to help you. We're concerned about you." To establish rapport, I gave a brief testimony about my own drug background. I didn't mention Nancy's recent experience, wanting to hold her story for reinforcement if needed.

We invited Mary to sit down and tell us about the type of drugs she used. She began to talk and told us she had started by sniffing transmission "go"—paint solvents, lacquer thinner, and glue. From these she had developed a speech impediment, her hair was beginning to fall out, and skin eruptions were occurring on various parts of her body.

She told us she had gone from inhaling solvent fumes to using marijuana, and from marijuana to LSD. I asked Mary why she was doing it. Her reply was, "It's just groovy, just great! All my friends are doing it." When I told her the possibilities of her flipping out, becoming mentally deranged, she insisted that it would never happen to her.

As we talked further of her drug life and drug experiences I asked Mary where she got money to buy her drugs. She looked straight at me and said, "Come on, reverend, you're not that square!"

"Are you prostituting your body to get money for drugs for yourself and your friends?" I asked.

"Yes," she readily admitted.

Looking hard at that twelve-year-old girl, I froze. Nancy and Barbara sat with mouths open in surprise at seeing a twelve-year-old confessed prostitute before their eyes. Then we explained to Mary why we were there, that we wanted her to come with us, that we would find her a place away from her home and friends. "We want to help you overcome this drug problem, Mary," Barbara pleaded. Mary said she was not ready to give up drugs because she liked them too much.

This retort ignited my mind, and I said, "Yes, you like your drugs a lot, but do you know that Jesus Christ loves you and he died for you?" She gave me a strange look making me ask, "You do believe in God, don't you, Mary?"

"Yeah, I believe in God."

"What about Jesus Christ?"

She said, "Oh, I think Jesus Christ is a groovy guy."

I replied, "Yes, he's groovy all right. He's so groovy he took our sins upon himself on the cross and there he died for you! Mary, if you were the only person in the world, hooked on drugs, Jesus Christ would have gone to the cross for you!"

Then Nancy shared her recent conversion experience as we tried to help Mary see her need of Christ. Although she appeared appreciative, Mary was not ready that night to yield her life to the Lord. Before we left, I asked Mary and her mother if we could pray with them.

They agreed, and I prayed that Jesus Christ would make himself known to Mary so she could experience his love and find new life in him.

After we prayed, Mary looked up and said, "Ah, ain't that cute." She said it not at all facetiously, but sincerely. I thought it probably was the first time anyone had prayed aloud for Mary in her hearing. As we left I again asked Mary to come with us, but she declined saying she would let us know by the weekend if she decided to accept our offer of a new place to stay. Our hearts were heavy as we left Mary's house, knowing she would go back to her drugs, and to her debauched life. Our hearts, like her mother's, were broken.

That night I had difficulty sleeping. After tossing for some time, I dropped to my knees beside the bed, crying for God to help young people see they were destroying themselves with drugs. Their minds, bodies, and souls were being wasted, and their eternal doom was certain unless Christ became real to them. Ruth awakened and I told her what deep disappointment I had felt that night about the tragedy of Mary's life.

Ruth put her head in her hands and said, "What is our world going to be like when Jackie reaches the age of twelve?" With tears streaming down my face, I could only look at her and shake my head, not knowing what to say.

The next night Glenn Bondurant called to say they now had a girls' halfway house. Momentarily confused, I couldn't imagine what he was talking about. He quickly explained that a friend of ours, Stan Frederick, a young Baptist minister, gave up his apartment to live and work with us at our boys' halfway house. Since he had paid rent ahead for three months on his lovely apartment, he said we could use it as a halfway house for girls.

Even better, a young college graduate, Patsy Duggan, volunteered to come and work with us in the Turning Point ministry. So on Thursday we moved Patsy and Nancy into the apartment and thus started our girls' halfway house. On Friday night Mary called and asked if we could accept her into our halfway house program. I called Patsy, who soon picked up Mary and her belongings, and settled her into the apartment halfway house—but not for long.

Mary let it be known that the halfway house was run by squares. The no smoking and no dating rules really turned her off. She just wasn't ready to give up her old life. We had made it clear that if she came into our program, she would have to give up smoking and adhere to our other rules for eighteen months. After the second or third day Mary began acting up.

Knowing she was annoyed about something, I called her into the counseling room and talked to her about what was happening in her life, and tried to help her understand the counseling program. She said she just didn't dig the discipline. I told her she was going to need discipline if her life was ever going to amount to anything more than a streetwalker or a dope addict. She wouldn't listen, but kept saying, "I want to go home. I want to go home. I've done too much wrong to come into the program!"

I knew Mary was lying. She didn't want to conform to the program. She didn't want to untwist her life. She felt as many young drug users do: they must have one more run, one more good time before they stop. That night I asked Mary if she would pray with me. I told her we didn't want her to go back on drugs because we loved her. I asked her to bow her head with me before she made any decision to stay or leave. She consented.

Extending my hand, I felt gratified when Mary grasped it. The feel of her bony fingers, small and fragile, made me think, How could anybody take advantage of a kid like this? Aloud I prayed, "Lord, help Mary. She's in the dark and doesn't know which way to go. Help her to know that we love her and care for her. In Jesus' name. Amen."

Mary looked up and said, "Vince, please don't think badly of me, but I want to go home, back to my mother." We notified Mary's mother that Mary was returning home. We never saw her again. Her mother told us Mary had flipped out on LSD, and had lost all contact with reality. She had to be admitted to a state mental hospital.

The following few weeks I traveled with Reverend Denver Smoot, speaking at various clubs and groups in many parts of Florida. There were unusually responsive meetings of Rotarians, Optimists, Lions, and Kiwanians. But the most overwhelming experience I had was when I spoke before the Miami Kiwanis Club. It is the largest club in the state, and after I had shared some of my experiences involving my work with drug users, the vast crowd rose as one man in a standing ovation. They even extended an invitation for me to join their club. Strangest of all was the fact that while I talked about what Christ meant to me, several businessmen responded with fervently uttered "Praise the Lord" and "Amen."

Through that speaking engagement I became acquainted with Mr. Bill Brazil, now a good friend of mine. He asked me to speak at the Florida Broadcasters' Association Convention in Key Biscayne. I accepted, learning that Mr. Brazil is general manager of WTVJ, Channel 4, in Miami. After I spoke to the FBA Convention in the Key Biscayne Hotel, I saw people leave the auditorium with tears in their eyes. I had told them of many dangers facing our nation's youth, and of the one hope—Jesus Christ.

At the end of my talk Mr. Brazil said to me, "Vince, it was good to hear from someone who knows his topic not only from the drug scene but from the Christian viewpoint!" Later that week I received a call from Channel 4 asking if I would do a talk program with interviewer Larry King. I jumped at the chance!

Many people saw the interview Larry King had with me. This exposure made things really begin to happen for our Turning Point ministry. Young people with drug hangups began calling for help and information to overcome their problems. Mothers, fathers, sisters and brothers telephoned us for information to help family members and friends find relief from drugs.

Dr. Rose, pastor of Miami Shores Presbyterian Church, invited me to speak to his huge congregation—so large it required two worship services each Sunday morning. I did so, simply telling those great audiences what Christ had done in my life, how he is changing my life, and how he leads me to many turning points. In the first service I felt greatly inspired and people received my message with warmth.

However, after I delivered my message in the second service people came forward to introduce themselves. While shaking hands and greeting people I noticed a distinguished-looking gentleman and his wife approaching. The man stuck out his hand and said, "Vince, I want to know more about Jesus Christ. How do you get this thing you talked about this morning?" Seeing the long line of well-wishers behind the couple, I suggested that the man and woman might be seated and I would be with them as soon as possible. They sat down, and I continued to greet new friends. Many told me about children or grandchildren fooling around with dangerous drugs. One registered nurse said she knew what I was talking about when I mentioned deformed babies born to drug addicts. She worked in a private hospital and had seen babies born to LSD users—babies hopelessly crippled!

As the line dwindled to nothing, I turned to the couple waiting for me. Mr. and Mrs. Winters and I talked a few moments, then I asked, "You want to know more about Jesus Christ?" The man nodded affirmatively and his eyes filled with tears.

I asked his wife if she too was interested in knowing more about Christ. She grabbed her husband's hand in a gesture of togetherness and replied, "Yes, I too want to know Jesus Christ!" They had a sixteen-year-old daughter with them, so I asked her if she wanted to know more about Christ.

She hesitated a moment then said, "No, not right at this moment."

Mr. Winters told me about their son who travels for Youth for Christ. It seems he had an experience similar to mine and had allowed Jesus Christ to become his personal Savior. Until today the father couldn't understand his son's enthusiasm. He said to me, "My son is a born-again Christian. He tells us in his letters of his many wonderful experiences with the Lord." This fiftyish-looking man wanted the same experience known by his son.

In that magnificient church-edifice that Sunday morning, I led Mr. and Mrs. Winters off to one side, then helped them pray to receive Christ. Both of them then and there accepted Christ as Lord and Savior! They left the building with smiling faces and radiant appearances.

We were invited to many groups and churches to talk only about drugs, but we felt strongly that we should present a message of Christian hope and evangelism. In just about every church service in which we spoke, five to twenty-five persons responded to the invitation to receive Jesus Christ.

At one church in Lake Wales a most unusual experience occurred as God worked mightily yet—to us—mysteriously. The service lasted nearly two hours, and in that building seating not more than 150 persons, dozens of young men and women attending a nearby college rededicated themselves and sought to place their lives more fully in God's will. What was to have been a drug talk had turned into the beginnings of spiritual revival.

At another time, I spoke at a private school in central Florida. When I finished, the student body gave a standing ovation, indicating I had told it like it was. My partner, Denver Smoot, asked the principal if we could have a rap session that night. The principal said, "Yes, by all means." To our surprise, about seventy-five students showed up.

That night Pandora's cupboard was opened as young people aired their frustrations. Some ten students asked to talk with me privately, sharing their drug problems. Many said they wanted to stop using drugs, that they didn't know why they used them. I told them I would be back on Saturday to talk with them.

On Saturday, Denver and I went back to the school. Each of us took students into separate rooms to rap with them. There we heard unbelievable-yet-true stories of parents who showered their children with money but cared nothing for them. They were allowed to live whatever kind of life they chose, with no guidance or sense of right or wrong. Some fifteen- to eighteen-year-olds lived lives not experienced by many persons in their mid-thirties.

One girl confessed to having a tremendous sex problem. She said she had committed fornication since she was thirteen and now could see nothing wrong with sexual encounter with a boy if she liked him. I asked her if she believed in God, if she thought God was pleased with her kind of life. She said she didn't really know if there was a God! She said her father was a traveling salesman who never took much interest in his children. He never taught them about God.

I asked her if there was something inside that made her want to look up and find God and acknowledge him. She admitted there was a slight spark inside that made her want to worship something. I told her this was God's way of helping us to know he is God, to want to seek him, and to allow him to make himself known to us.

Carefully I explained how God sent Jesus Christ to this earth to live among men, to go to the cross, to die for man's sins. She thought the story was beautiful, but said she only wished it could be true. Again, I used my own life as an illustration, telling her how wonderfully God had changed my life and made me a new creation in Christ. I shared 2 Corinthians 5:17 with her: "Therefore, if any one is in Christ, he is a new creation; the old has passed away, behold, the new has come."

I told her that everything in my life was new and that she too could experience this change in her life if she wanted Jesus Christ to transform her life. She said, "Vince, I don't want anything less than that!" We prayed in that small office where I counseled her. There she received Jesus Christ as her Savior!

Moments later a young Jewish woman strolled into the room. She wore a fedora hat and men's jewelry. She said, "You know, Vince, I heard what you said about Jesus Christ at the end of your speech yesterday." I shared with her about how wonderfully Christ had changed my life, then I asked her what she thought about Jesus. She replied, "Oh, I think he was a wonderful person."

"Do you believe he was the Son of God?" I pursued.

She responded, "Being a Jew, I find this is contrary to what I was taught as a young child."

"Nevertheless, do you believe in him?"

"Yes, I do," she admitted. I asked her if she would like to dedicate her life to Jesus Christ that day and she said yes. I led her in a simple prayer which she prayed very sincerely: "Dear Jesus, I have sinned against you and I now ask your forgiveness for all my sins. Please come into my life and make me a Christian. In your name I pray. Amen." After that simple prayer, the Jewish girl lifted her head in a solemn, slow-motion way, looked directly at me, and said, "Groovy, groovy, groovy." And with that she walked from the room.

The next two persons who came into the counseling room that day rejected Jesus Christ. They felt they could find happiness and peace through a better relationship with their parents. I suggested to them that perhaps they could have a happy life, but Jesus Christ alone could give them the ultimate life they sought. Still they refused.

Just before Denver and I left the school that day into my room marched the little Jewish girl. She shook my hand, saying, "Thanks, Vince. Thanks a lot. It was a groovy experience and I'm going to hang on to Jesus. I'm going to start reading my Bible!"

The four-hundred-mile drive home seemed only a couple of hours long. I could hardly wait to tell Ruth about what God had done at that private school, and to see who else I could help to have a "groovy experience."

3

Peace, Brother, Peace

The next few weeks were extremely busy ones. I was gone from home three or four days each week while speaking and enlisting support for our Turning Point ministry. Ruth grew more lonely, and I became upset because I could not spend more time with her and our growing son, Jackie. More and more, my prayers turned to the hope of soon having a halfway house where young people we met on the streets and talked to in jails could be taken for rehabilitation and help.

Not only did I ask God for a halfway house, but also for finances to operate it. I knew the expenses would be staggering, but I was sure that God could provide friends with the means to support such a venture. I talked with Denver Smoot about the need I felt. I shared my hope with Glenn Bondurant—and with anyone who would listen. It became my chief burden and concern as I continued to pray about it.

Glenn had acquired a one-family dwelling where he housed three or four men—off the street and off drugs. In that environment he tried to present the gospel of Christ to them. However, we had no trained supervision and the house was only a temporary facility from which Glenn knew he would soon have to move.

Glenn and I began to talk, dream, and plan for a half-way house in the Fort Lauderdale area. I refused many speaking engagements offered to me, especially on weekends. I wanted to be near my family, and also, I spent weekend nights working with youth in the coffeehouse and on the streets. Here were people with such great needs—people like Bruce.

Someone asked me to visit Bruce, a young man who supposedly had received a revelation from God to jump off a bridge and die—a sacrifice for the world. I honestly thought my informant was kidding me about Bruce's savior complex. But I went to his home, and met his mother who told me Bruce was in his room. She said he had been acting strangely all day, so I knew I would have difficulty establishing rapport with him.

I told her to let me go into her son's room by myself. I hoped to establish my friendliness before he could be turned off. Opening his door, I crouched low, walked in with a wide smile on my face, and with both hands gave the peace sign. As I approached him, I said, "Peace, brother, peace!"

His reply was, "Hey, baby, come on in and dig the vibs." His stereo was playing as loudly as it could go, so I put my forefingers in my ears and yelled for him to lower the volume so I could hear him.

"What?" he shouted above the din.

"Lower the box!" I yelled again, fingers in my ears for emphasis.

"Okay, daddy-o," he laughed, moving to tone down the noise. I put out my hand and he shook it, indicating he had accepted and acknowledged me without knowing who I was. I told him I worked with House of Ichthus

Turning Point. He said, "Oh, yeah, I heard about you. You're some pretty dynamite people and you help a lot of kids hung up on dope."

I acknowledged that was our business and he replied, "Some of my friends have gone to you for help and counseling." I knew our friendship was solidly established.

Without hesitation I said, "I heard something happened to you the other night. Do you want to tell me about it?"

He said, "What do you mean?"

"Someone told me you went swimming."

"Oh, yeah. That was a pretty wild experience. God told me to jump off the bridge and drown myself for the world." I asked Bruce how he had gotten this message from God. He pointed to the radio. I asked him if he was listening to a religious service. He emphatically said no. When I asked him how he had received the message, he said, "The DJ, man, the disc jockey!" I asked him to explain himself.

Patiently, as if to a child, Bruce unfolded his story. "I got little bits and pieces from what the DJ was saying and from some of the songs played by the acid rock groups. I started to take notes, and this is what I got: to take my Bible down to the water and jump in. So I did. I took my Bible and jumped into the water."

I asked him if he believed God gave him that message.

Soberly, Bruce replied, "No, I didn't get it from God. God gave it to the DJ, and he gave it to me."

"Who does God speak through?" I queried.

"People," he replied.

"That's right. What kind of people?"

"Christians." When I asked Bruce if he thought the

people who played this kind of music were Christians he said no.

"Well," I pursued, "if they're not Christians, then who are they of? Whose work do they do?"

"Man, they're of Satan, that's right." With that, I asked him to get his Bible and together we looked up scriptures showing that Jesus Christ is the Savior of the world, that he alone paid sin's price and died on the cross to redeem us. I showed Bruce John 1:36, where John the Baptist spoke of Jesus as the "Lamb of God," indicating Christ is the sacrifice for man's sin. Together we looked at John 3:16 and read, "For God so loved the world that he gave his only begotten Son, that whosoever believeth in him should not perish, but have everlasting life."

I asked Bruce if he was God's son and he said no. I asked him who was God's Son and he said, "Jesus Christ."

Encouraged, I went on, "That's right. And through him, through his death on the cross, we can become sons of God." I read John 1:12 to help Bruce better understand. "But as many as received him, to them gave he power to become the sons of God, even to them that believe on his name." Then I asked him, "How would you like to really become a son of God and brother to Jesus Christ?"

His eyes lighted up. "Man, that would be out of sight!"

I asked, "Do you really mean it? Let's forget the jive talk and everything else. Would you really like to know Jesus Christ as your personal Savior?"

He looked at me and said, "Vince, I think that would be great if it could really happen."

I shared with him how God had changed my life, and before I finished my life's story sensed the Holy Spirit working in him. I said, "Come on, Bruce, let's kneel right now and you pray with me." Moments later Bruce accepted Christ as his Lord and Savior!

Immediately he jumped to his feet and went to his mother and father to share his good news. He threw his arms around his startled mother, then put out his hand in a manly gesture toward his father. He apologized to both parents for all the misery and heartache he had caused them.

I advised Bruce before I left to get into church and establish fellowship with other Christians. I told him if he didn't, he probably would go back out into the streets and start using drugs all over again. He assured me he would attend church services, and that he would come every Thursday night to the House of Ichthus Coffee House where drug encounter sessions are held.

Returning home, I rejoiced at how easily Bruce had received transformation of his mind and life. While I mused on the wonder of Christian conversion and the new birth process, the telephone rang. Glenn Bondurant wanted me to go with him to Fort Lauderdale, a twenty-five-minute drive from my house. He said some friends of his were having some kind of spiritual trouble, and that he would explain it to me on our way there.

I drove over to the House of Ichthus—run by Glenn and his wife Barbara—and Glenn and I hurried to Ft. Lauderdale where his young friends lived. Glenn clued me in as we drove: the two fellows claimed to have a revelation from Christ about the geographical location of the new Jerusalem.

Admitted into the house, we quickly learned from the two young men—professing Christians—that they had been reading, studying, and fasting, seeking signs and a message from God. They claimed God had chosen them to be prophets in their area. Glenn and I sat back and listened as they vented their story. Having prayed just before entering the house, Glenn and I perceived a spirit of uneasiness, of dissonance, as we sat there.

Donald, one of the young men, told us the Holy Spirit had revealed to him the fact that Anthony—the other youth—and a girl named Jane were to be priest and priestess of a new order. Donald, too, would be a priest. God was resurrecting his new church and they were to be children of the elect. Glenn and I looked at each other as Donald unfolded his story. Seeing our unbelief, Donald said accusingly, "What's the matter? You're looking at me as though you think I'm crazy!"

Quickly I told him we didn't think so, but I was curious to know what else he might say. He said the new Jerusalem was going to be right in Fort Lauderdale, and people would come from miles around to join his new church—the Church of the Elect!

The two men had told us Jane was expected to come over, and while Donald was talking, Anthony jumped up and shouted, "Jane is going to be here in three minutes!" We waited three minutes, but Jane did not appear. Anthony said, "No, I'm wrong. It's going to be another five minutes." Again, after five minutes, no Jane. Then Anthony insisted it would be a minute-and-a-half. Still no Jane.

Glenn and I decided the best thing we could do would be to leave Donald and Anthony alone, but to assure them of our prayers. They were too mystified to be rational and logical, so we told them we would appreciate their staying away from the coffeehouse with their new theology. We assured them we still wanted their friendship but were rejecting their concept of the "new church."

Soon after that, both young men began talking against the coffeehouse and our ministry. They berated ministers of the gospel and churches where genuine Christian experience was proclaimed and practiced. A few days later we learned that Anthony had suffered a mental collapse and was in a state hospital. We realized that Satan had deluded those young men, sincere though they were. Fortunately, Jane, who was to have become priestess in the new setup, also became aware of this deception and admitted the revelation came not from God, but from Satan. Don later confessed it had to be from Satan since nothing good had come from it.

The next few weeks we concentrated on our jail ministry in Miami and Fort Lauderdale. This phase of our work has led many young men into our drug encounter groups where they learned firsthand of the power of God. One day we had a group of new fellows who had not heard my testimony. I was asked to share it with them, something I'm always glad to do.

The results that day were astonishing. About seven young men asked me to talk with them in the counseling room, and there I led four black youths into a saving knowledge of Jesus Christ. One young man, Charlie, said, "I'm facing a five-year rap. Now I know that Jesus Christ is living in my heart. Whether I beat this rap or not, I'm still going to hang on to him."

Jerry, another youth, said he was going to hold fast to Jesus Christ no matter what came, whether he became depressed or not. Both Jerry and Charlie began to seriously study the Bible. Soon they began to pray for other inmates in the prison. One fellow, Willie, had his bail set at $100,-000. Jerry and Charlie began to pray for Willie, but Willie laughed, "Oh, man, that's just kid stuff. It doesn't work!"

Jerry and Charlie continued to pray for Willie. And when he returned that evening from court, Willie shouted, "Man, guess what! My bail was dropped from $100,000 to $1,500!" Jerry and Charlie just smiled at each other. This experience brought a change in Willie. The next time the tall, six-footer was in our drug encounter group he asked to speak to me in our counseling room.

There he told me about his homelife; his parents were divorced. His father was an alcoholic. His mother had to work in a sweatshop. Willie had little education, but wanted to better himself. He asked if he could have the same faith in God that Jerry and Charlie had.

I said, "Certainly you can, Willie!" Then I explained the plan of salvation. He immediately responded and accepted Jesus Christ. From that experience, two other young men came and asked me about Jesus Christ. I rejoiced that our drug encounter sessions were having such rich results.

One fellow, Mike, had been in just about every program going for drug addicts: Daytop, Synanon—but not one of them worked for him. He told me he had played in the Synanon band. One day when he had the strong urge to buy drugs he took a clarinet from the instrument warehouse, sold it at a pawnshop, and bought himself a fix.

He told me, "Vince, there must be more to life than rules and regulations."

I explained, "For a person to experience life and really know life to the fullest he should know and receive Jesus Christ as his personal Savior."

Earnestly, Mike looked at me and said, "Man, if I was sure it would work, I'd make that dedication right now! Do you really think it's possible for me to become a Christian and be drug free?"

I said, "Mike, just because you do receive Jesus Christ as your Lord and Savior, you will not immediately solve all your problems: Your problems will still be there. But what Jesus Christ does do is to give power to the individual to be able to say no to temptation when confronted by problems. A Christian's life is a life of prayer—especially for guys like you and me. We have to be constantly in prayer and not be in the environment of drugs. We have to be involved in something constructive."

I paused, then added, "Personally, I got very heavily involved in the work of my church, working with young people who had problems at home. I took them on hikes and outings, things like that."

Mike looked thoughtful, then asked, "You mean you have to give your life in order to save your life?"

"That's exactly the way it is, Mike. Jesus Christ gave his life to save the world—you and me."

"You know, Vince," Mike said slowly, "I think you're on to something!"

I pressed him, feeling the time was right. "Would you like to make your dedication now to Christ? Would you like to ask him to come into your life?"

Starting to cry, Mike swallowed and said, "Yes, I would like to. I think that's the only way out for me." And right there in the Dade County Jail, Miami, Florida, Mike—hardened drug user that he had been—received and accepted Jesus Christ as his own Lord and Savior.

I made it clear to him that his acceptance did not mean he would be freed from the penalty imposed by the court. I assured him that God would give him strength and grace to face whatever lay before him. I further assured him of my prayers that spiritual strength would be given to him.

As with most young men who make their dedication to Christ under similar circumstances, Mike acknowledged he knew this was no guarantee that he would get off the hook or beat the rap. But he was confident of God's help and love.

4

Running from God!

One evening, just before I was to leave for drug rehabilitation sessions at the Sign of the Fish Coffee House in Coral Cables, the telephone rang. Answering it, I recognized the voice of Mrs. Smoot. She told me about a young man named Jim, who was looking for her husband, Denver Smoot. At that time Denver was serving as chaplain abroad a Caribbean Sea cruise ship. So Mrs. Smoot gave Jim the name and telephone number of Eston Hunter, a probation and parole officer in Dade County. He is also a drug specialist in the probation and parole office.

Jim called Eston, who told him to go to the Sign of the Fish. I jotted down Jim's name given to me by Mrs. Smoot. That night I walked into the room where the encounter session was held, handed Eston the slip of paper, and asked him if Jim had showed up. Eston pointed toward a young fellow in black pants and a blue shirt. The young man was heavily tanned, yet looked sickly. He was bent over in a kind of half-crouch. "There he is," said Eston.

During the encounter session, Jim contributed little, but afterward I introduced myself to him and told him my story. Then Jim told me some of his own experiences. He said Christ was calling him to get off drugs and to give himself to the Lord. Yet he said he didn't understand it all.

He said, "I found myself one time in a cellar in Brooklyn, New York. There was a book in the cellar—a Bible—from which I read many passages like, 'He who calls upon the name of the Lord shall be saved.' 'He who comes unto me, I will in no wise cast out.' "

I knew without a doubt that Jim was running from God. He said that at nine years of age he was abandoned by his parents and was placed in a school for truants. At thirteen, he broke away from that school and, along with friends, held up a small-town California bank. Caught again and put into jail until he was seventeen, he finally was adopted by a Christian family. Although he received much instruction and guidance, Jim decided Christianity wasn't for him.

He liked a fast life and big money, so, at nineteen, he told his foster mother he appreciated all she had done for him and set out to make his own way in life. Knowing the Spanish language well, Jim often traveled into Mexico, bought large quantities of marijuana and smuggled it back over the border into the States. He wholesaled the drug for several years.

He also lived in several South American countries where marijuana was so strong that, according to Jim, after smoking some of it he would vomit. He said that marijuana grown in Panama was so powerful that "two or three puffs and it'll take the socks right off your feet!"

Eventually Jim became involved with the Syndicate and also smuggled and sold guns to revolutionary groups. Yet he never took any drug stronger than marijuana. He felt that anyone who used heroin was likely to end up on a slab or as a loser in life—and that wasn't his game. His game, he insisted, was to make big money and retire at an early age.

So at twenty, Jim had a new Cadillac, bought two- to three-hundred-dollar suits, and paid cash for everything he bought. He was strictly big time. This was the way he lived: girls, money, liquor, marijuana, and no time to fritter away. To him, time was important and he tried to get all the kicks he could from life.

Jim made so many trips between the United States and Mexico, Jamaica, and Trinidad, that he began to fear he would be caught. He lay low for about five months, then, running short of cash, decided to sell heroin to make fast money. Of course, handling the drug made him want to try it. At first he took just an occasional buzz, not intending to become hooked. But he wound up with a fantastic habit.

Running from California law enforcement officers, he went to New York to stay with friends. His addiction increased and every effort Jim made to get out ended up as a dead-end street. He even went to a program with a Christian emphasis where one of the directors said, "Jim, if you don't give your heart to Christ, you're going to wind up dead." Jim ran again, moving deeper into the drug scene, finally moving to Puerto Rico.

There he bought heroin in many novelty shops, often right over the counter. Or he would give a pusher the money and take the drug right out on the street corner where guys and girls hung out. There he could easily get a set of works —a hypodermic needle, or an eyedropper and needle.

During his two-year stay in Puerto Rico Jim often wanted to drop his drug habit, but he couldn't. Finally he received a letter from his foster mother urging him to come home, even telling him God was calling him to come home again. She said she was praying for him and gave him the telephone number of a man he should call when he got back to the United States. That number belonged to Denver Smoot!

Denver had spoken at a workshop where Jim's aunt heard him. She in turn gave Denver's telephone number to Jim's mother. Jim carefully weighed the possibility of coming to Florida to try to shake the drug habit. One evening after stealing some money, instead of buying a fix, Jim bought a plane ticket and landed in Florida. That night I saw him in the coffeehouse, bent over and sick, withdrawing from heroin.

Knowing Jim needed a place to stay, I found myself praying, "Oh, God, if only we had a halfway house we could take Jim to, where he could find Christ and regain his health. Oh, if only we had a Turning Point Halfway House." My throat tightened as I thought of what Jim was going through. I knew what it was like, knew he needed love, understanding, and compassion. He was a fine-looking fellow with a winning personality. I enjoyed talking with him even though he was withdrawing from heroin and kicking his sixty-dollar-a-day habit.

When the other youths left the rehab group, Jim and I went into another room and talked privately. I asked him, "What do you want? What can we do for you?"

Back came his reply, "I want to be free! I want to get rid of this drug hangup. I want to stop using drugs and find God, because I feel like he's going to bomb me if I don't give myself to him." I asked him what he knew about Christianity. He replied, "I know quite a bit about the Bible. My foster mother is a tremendous Christian and I was raised in Sunday school to a certain extent. I've been running from Christ though, and now I want to stop running."

Now that he was willing to turn to Christ and away from drugs, what would I do with him? With a young son at home, I didn't feel I should take Jim there. Eston Hunter had four children of his own in their mobilehome, so that was out of the question. I know, I thought, I'll call Glenn Bondurant. But no one answered the telephone.

I decided to take Jim to Fort Lauderdale, a forty-five-minute drive from where we were in Coral Gables. Since I had been in Florida only a few months at that time, I knew Glenn would know many more possible places for Jim to stay than I did. Jim lay doubled up in the back seat, experiencing the pains with which I was so familiar. Every time he moaned, I felt the pain in my own stomach.

We drove straight to the House of Ichthus, but it was closed. I tried to call Glenn's house but no one answered. Several more times I called after waiting many minutes. Finally, as I was about to give up, Glenn answered the phone. He said he knew of no place we could take Jim, since all available places were already filled. I became desperate.

"Glenn, we have to help this young man, because he is going through living hell!" At this, Glenn said he would be where we were in five minutes. When he and Barbara arrived, I introduced them to Jim, who still lay on the back seat in agony. One look at Jim, and Glenn remembered a Nazarene minister, Reverend Jeter, who might take him in. But when we called the Jeter home the wife informed Glenn that her husband was away on a speaking engagement.

However, when Glenn mentioned our predicament, she offered Jim a place to stay for as long as he needed it. I thought, Here's a woman who doesn't even know us, yet she's willing to open her home to a junkie who's kicking the habit and to people she knows very little about.

We drove straight to the Jeter home, where we were warmly received. Jim was starting to have the dry retches, so we got him under a hot shower. Then we alternated the water from hot to cold, back to hot. This relieved most of the cramps and pain. After Jim's shower, Mrs. Jeter made him eat some toast and tea. Then she led him to the room where for three-and-a-half days he would go through agony and torment withdrawing from heroin.

I sent Glenn and his wife home, and prepared for a long nightwatch. Mrs. Jeter retired for the night after we had prayer together. I began reading the Bible, but had to fight sleep at that late hour. I turned on the television, opened a bottle of soda, walked the floor, trying to stay awake. I catnapped, awakening each time Jim tried to get up to leave. Several times he insisted he couldn't make it, that he wanted to go out and get a fix.

I told him God had brought him a long way, that this was the time to find out who God really was, and what God wanted him to do with his life. Tears of remorse came to Jim's eyes, regret over the agony he had caused so many people. He took another hot-and-cold shower and returned to bed.

Glenn relieved me when morning came, and I went home to sleep all day, returning to the Jeter residence that night. For some time after Glenn left, Mrs. Jeter, Jim, and I talked about spiritual matters. Jim took in the whole conversation until nearly midnight, when Mrs. Jeter went to her room. He said his pains were less severe, but the cramps were returning. We went through the hot-and-cold shower again, then Jim lay down to sleep.

I've noted that a junkie kicking the habit can nap for about an hour at a time, then he wakes up for four hours fighting the pain. This is called the "gaps." Jim got up three or four times that night, but found his pains less severe as time went by. By the third day he felt better, and the fourth day he ate a good meal. That night I felt we could burden Mrs. Jeter no longer, yet did not know where we could take Jim. I had a strong urge to take him to my house—against my will.

I'd made a vow before moving to Florida never to take a junkie in to live in my home. Yet, now it seemed that God wanted me to do that very thing. Throughout the night as I watched over Jim, I thought of what such a move might mean to Ruth and Jackie. My prayers were troubled ones, seeking relief from my dilemma, but finding none.

When I arrived home the next morning, I noticed that Ruth had been crying. Holding her close, I asked what was wrong. She said, "Vince, I had the feeling last night that Christ was so very near to me in our home." Right then I blurted out my feeling that Jim should come to stay at our house. To my amazement, Ruth readily agreed he could stay until we got our halfway house.

That evening I picked up Jim and we drove to Coral Gables for an encounter session at the Sign of the Fish Coffee House. Jim participated, telling how junkies like to exaggerate about using more drugs than they really do. Jim told this for the benefit of some newcomers to the program who were bragging about all the types of drugs they used. Finally we headed home to Hollywood—where I lived.

On the way I told him, "You know, Jim, when I came to Florida, I vowed never to take a junkie into my home.

Two nights ago while praying about where to take you, I thought of every place but my own home. Then I felt God wanted me to take you there." I told him about Ruth's deep spiritual experience with Christ and how she and I agreed that Jim should stay with us until our halfway house materialized. I warned him that as the first male junkie to stay at our home, his behavior would determine whether others found our home open or closed to them.

Jim's head was buried in his hands, and he wept. "Vince," he said, "One of my main concerns has been whether or not I could stay with you. I enjoyed staying with other people, but you know what I'm thinking and feeling. And this is the kind of help I need. I need people who understand."

I replied, "Jim, we understand, but above all we love you. We want you to get straightened out." I explained that he needn't get a job until his health returned, until he'd gained some weight.

Well, he gained weight all right, Jim just about ate us out of house and home. Every night before going to bed, Jim poured a half-quart of milk over a box of Frosted Flakes for a bedtime snack. Then in the night he'd wake up and fix himself some sandwiches. I began to think I'd have to get another job to buy the extra groceries we needed. But it was good to see his appetite and health increase.

Jim's main problem was with smoking. Often he'd ask me for fifty cents to buy a pack of cigarettes. The first few times he asked, I gave him the money. Then one day just as I was about to leave the house, Jim said, "Vince, how about half a buck so I can buy myself some weeds?"

It so happened that fifty cents was all I had in my pocket, so I said, "Jim, it's either a packet of cigarettes for you or a half-gallon of milk for you and Jackie. You're not getting any cigarettes, and don't ask me for any more money."

Jim knew he had to either give up cigarettes or go out and get a job. He didn't ask me for more money, but one day I saw a pack of cigarettes in his shirt pocket and asked him where he got them. He replied that he'd ripped them from the corner grocery store. Angered that Jim would stoop to petty thievery, I stood up, handed him fifty cents, and said, "Jim, here's fifty cents. You go and pay that man for the pack of cigarettes."

Jim asked me not to make him go back and pay, so I told him if he ever did it again I'd go there personally and rat on him. He promised never to do it again, and to my knowledge he didn't.

Occasionally I had to leave Ruth and Jackie in the house with Jim. During those times, I often thought how I, as a drug addict, could never be trusted. Yet, here I was trusting Jim to be alone in my home with my wife and son. Strangely, Jesus Christ gave me the confidence that everything would be all right. Ruth always told me upon my return home that Jim was a perfect gentleman. Moreover, Jim and Jackie became the best of buddies. I often found that young men who came to us quickly identified with little Jackie and loved to play with him.

One evening Jim and I talked about the day he had called Denver Smoot's house, about why he came to us at Turning Point. I refreshed his memory about how God led him to seek help for his addiction, about his desire to know Christ. I said, "Well, how about it, Jim.

48

How about asking Christ to come into your life so you can know him in a very personal way?"

Jim replied, "Vince, I don't want to be pushed into this. I want to think about it, and when I do make my decision, I want to really mean it." He became emphatic. "I've known so-called Christian people before. They're wonderful as long as you're not a Christian and they want you to accept Christ, but after you accept Christ, they drop you like a hot potato. I don't want that to happen here, and if you do drop me like a hot potato, I want enough strength to stand on my own two feet."

I acknowledged his right to think the way he did, but added, "Any time you want to know Christ as your Lord and Savior, and you want to make that dedication to him, don't hesitate to let me know."

Jim soberly replied, "Vince, when I feel that I want to, I'll let you know." I had the feeling he was being truthful.

The next day, Glenn had to appear in court to report on how one of our guys was doing. As Jim and I waited in the courtroom, I noticed the great number of youngsters there for hearings on various charges. My heart ached for them as I thought, Oh, if only we had that halfway house. How much we need a place where these young boys and girls could stay.

Soon Glenn and Arnett—the young ward—stood before the judge. Arnett faced a possible sentence of five years for narcotics use. The judge asked Glenn if Arnett was still using drugs. Glenn previously had told Arnett he'd have to be truthful, so he said as far as he knew, Arnett still used drugs. The judge asked Arnett and he admitted he was back on drugs. The judge remanded Arnett's bond, but withheld sentence and ordered pre-sentence investigation on Arnett. I was sad for Arnett, for he was one of those who confessed Christ when I preached at the Coral Ridge Presbyterian Church. Unfortunately, something had failed—but not Christ.

After the hearing Jim and I headed back toward Hollywood along I-95. I shared with Jim some experiences I'd had recently at the Hollywood Rock Festival, where Turning Point had ministered to hundreds. Jim laughed when I told him many kids had shied away from me because they thought I looked like a "narco"—a narcotics officer. With other young staffers tuned in and turned on to win souls I played it cool, and stayed near the gospel tent located a half- mile from the music area. There I handed out tracts and New Testaments to passersby.

A young man strolled over and I introduced myself to him. He very politely told me his name and we talked about the rock festival, pollution, Vietnam. Suddenly he said, "You're the group that's giving away food aren't you?" I nodded and he went on, "Man, you guys are doing a fantastic thing. A lot of people are talking about you."

He asked what church we represented. I said we were Christians simply trying to do a job for God. He said, "That's great. It's fantastic. That's the way it should be, not pushing any church in particular."

Picking up the cue, I asked, "Are you interested in spiritual matters?" He indicated he was, "to a certain degree." I asked, "To what degree do you know Jesus Christ?" He looked blank and asked what I meant, so I said, "If you have time, I'd like to explain four verses of Scripture to you."

He said he had plenty of time, so I shared with him Romans 3:23, 6:23, John 1:12, and Revelation 3:20. After quoting part of Revelation 3:20, I said, "This could be Jesus Christ knocking at your heart's door. Won't you open up your heart? You know, in order for Jesus Christ to come into your life, you need to open the door of your heart to let him come in. Christ is not a gate-crasher. You have to open the door to your life and let him in."

I sensed his interest, so continued, "We've been talking about love and peace today, Al. But this is what love and peace really means: knowing Jesus Christ as your Savior and accepting his pure love for your life." He began to show emotion, and I thought he might be high on dope or was putting on a front. I put my hand on his shoulder. "Al, how about it? Would you like to bow your head and ask Jesus Christ to come into your heart and forgive all your sins?"

He looked blank, so I said, "You have sinned, haven't you?"

"Oh, yeah. No doubt about that."

"Well, how about it? Let's really get into something."

He looked around, then said, "Okay, Vince. I'd like that." And right there in the tent at the Hollywood Speedway, where the huge rock festival was going on, the young hippie accepted Jesus Christ as his personal Savior.

After he confessed his sins to Christ and apologized for them, Al asked Christ to come into his life, praying the prayer of faith. Then he grabbed my hand, hugging and shaking it in elation. We walked together toward the main staging area, where he pointed toward thousands of young people grooving on pot, acid, and heroin, and listening to rock music. Al said, "Take what you've got to these people. They need it, just as much at I do." With that, he took the literature I had given him and went home.

That weekend at the rock festival, our gospel team heard marvelous reports of conversions and shared conversations with hundreds of youth hungry to know the solid Rock: Jesus Christ. Many hip youth insisted, "We dig Jesus Christ, but we don't dig the establishment—the people who come here and try to push their church down our throats." They pointed to little red stickers on our shirts on which were the words, "Smile. God loves you." Another group handed out little tags saying, "Jesus saves! Join the . . . Church!" Young people tore up those tags, but accepted our stickers gladly.

On Sunday, the last day of the festival, nearly one thousand New Testaments were given out to young people. As we gave out each testament we urged the receiver to read 1 Corinthians 13, the great love chapter. That week would remain long in my memory, I concluded to Jim as I turned the car into our driveway.

I shut off the engine, put my hand on Jim's shoulder, and said, "Jim, I feel the Lord wants you to accept him as Lord and Savior."

Dropping his head, he said, "Vince, I'm still not ready. I'm not sure what I want to do."

"Well, don't forget, Jim. There's an open invitation to you. Any time you feel you want to know Christ or you want to talk about it, call me—whether it's two o'clock in the morning or whenever." He said he appreciated my concern.

That evening after dinner, I prepared to go out for an appointment. Jim was going with me. I was in my bedroom, just putting on my trousers, when in walked Jim. He said,

"Vince, I want to know more about—Jesus Christ. I want to get saved and give my heart to him."

I responded, "That's wonderful, Jim. If you really mean it, let's kneel here beside my bed and pray." He and I knelt and Jim prayed to God, asking him to blot out his past, to erase all those bad memories of his younger life, his hatred of others, his insecurity. He asked God to forgive his thievery and lying. Jim asked Christ, reverently and lovingly, to come into his heart and make him a new person.

After he prayed that prayer of faith, I took Jim in my arms and held him tight in a grip of brotherly love and said, "God is really going to be with you, Jim. He's going to prepare you to do some pretty great things." And I meant it from the depths of my being.

5

Jim's Big Decision

Jim began to really dig into the Bible. As he read each chapter, he would write the entire portion in his own words. Then he would bring it to me and ask if it was a close enough paraprase. I soon learned that Jim was extremely intelligent. He spoke two languages fluently, and had some college background. He began to memorize and quote many Scripture verses.

But he also went through periods of deep depression. One day I asked him what was bugging him, knowing he was having difficulty finding a job. Every time he filled out an application, he noted it asked whether or not he had a police record or had ever been refused bond. He would become discouraged and tear up the application.

But he insisted this wasn't what was bothering him. Pressing him for an explanation, I finally got him to admit his problem. He said that a year-and-a-half earlier he had spent some time in West Palm Beach, Florida. While there, he forged several prescriptions for drug medications. He had passed these at a certain drugstore, but soon the police were notified and began to watch for Jim.

Learning there was a warrant for his arrest, Jim fled without being caught. But now that he was a Christian, Jim chafed under the awareness that he was wanted by the

West Palm Beach police. He asked me what he should do. I told him this was between him and Christ, but that I would pray with him for the right solution. Late into the night we discussed the matter. I told him it would be the easy thing to skip and leave Florida forever, but that only he himself could make the decision he'd have to live with the rest of his life.

I knew how difficult it would have been for me to make a decision that would have incriminated myself, and I felt sorry for him. Still, I told him not to make such a decision late at night when he was tired. We prayed earnestly for Jim's decision to be the right one, then went to bed. I slept very little, and Jim admitted to the same the next morning. Jim was making such splendid progress in his Christian life that I dreaded what might happen whichever way his decision went.

The next night, Thursday, Jim and I went to Fort Lauderdale to a drug rehab session. A large group of young people were there, among them a young black man, Cleve Bell. He had accepted Christ while in jail. Denver Smoot and Jerry Rutkin had visited Cleve and other addicts. Jerry had been a drug user for thirteen years before his conversion and subsequent work with Denver. Jerry's inspiring testimony helped Cleve to know what it meant to be free from drugs and soon Cleve, too, accepted Jesus Christ as Lord and Savior. Now out of jail for some time, Cleve was going straight.

Also in the group was Yve, a young girl who had lived with hippies for about a year. She had used every kind of drug available. She said that one day during a revival service in a Mennonite church she heard the evangelist speak of the saving power of Jesus, and she turned to

Christ. She broke with her old environment, turned off drugs, and became a beautiful person in Jesus Christ.

In the group with Yve was a Cuban girl named Maria, who was hooked on heroin. Maria had known Yve from school days and sought her understanding help when she desired to kick the habit. Yve agreed to go to Maria's house and stay with her while she withdrew from heroin. While there, Yve presented the way of salvation to Maria and Maria accepted Christ as Savior.

The outcome of this experience was fantastic. Maria told the rehab group that her withdrawal pains were much less severe after receiving Christ. She said she felt pure and good and clean again, and that she had been forgiven for her past. She asserted that the greatest thing about her experience with Christ was that she had regained her self-respect and once again believed in herself as a person— but a person only in Christ, not in her own strength.

When I asked Maria how long she had been off drugs, She replied, "Only about a week! But I can hardly wait till I can get into the ghetto area where my friends hang out and tell them about Christ."

I told her not to go back into that environment until she was sure she was strong enough to stay away from temptation. But she insisted she was now strong enough because she had Christ. I've known many young people who accepted Christ, but never grew spiritually strong. Going back to the old haunts, many quickly backslid and returned to drugs. I encouraged Maria not to go back if she felt the slightest temptation.

That night many youths shared their homelife hangups. Some were from poor neighborhoods, but others came from families with thirty-five-to-fifty-thousand-dollars-per-year incomes. Yet their homelife was terrible. They felt their parents cared more for things than they did for their children. We tried to listen objectively and inject seeds of understanding into the minds of the youngsters. We hoped to keep from widening the gaps they already felt. At the end of the session we prayed, then quickly dispersed.

After a restless night, I awoke with a splitting headache. I felt as though I was spinning, and was feverish. The weather had become chilly and Ruth unpacked woolen blankets and heavy sweaters. Under the warm covers, I decided to rest a little, hoping my symptoms would go away. Instead of getting better, I began to feel worse. I finally realized that I was really sick. The top of my head seemed about ready to explode.

I began to take aspirins and lots of liquids. However, the pain in my head increased and I began to cough. So I went to the doctor, who prescribed medication for my cold and fever. Since my drug addiction, I had scarcely taken even an aspirin, not wanting to trigger any latent desire for drugs. Now I looked at the bottle of medicine, read on the label that it contained codeine and feared what it might do to me.

In a flash, I recalled how I had drunk cough medicine when I was addicted. And this medicine was even stronger than that had been! Praying that it would not adversely affect me, I took the medicine as directed—four times a day—along with some pills the doctor prescribed. Within four or five days I was over the cold and severe flu, and I suffered no ill effects from the medication.

However, during the time of my illness, my son Jackie became quite ill, his temperature soaring to 105 degrees. Ruth and I became quite concerned about it and poor Jim was almost beside himself with helplessness. He loved our son as much as he would have loved one of his own.

Since our doctor was out of town, I wanted to take Jackie to the emergency ward at the hospital. Ruth insisted that I stay in bed, so I asked Jim, "Will you take Ruth and Jackie to the hospital, in my car?" He readily agreed. I told him, "You've never been out driving alone in a car before, since you've been here, Jim. Do you think you can go straight to the hospital and back without fooling around with anything, or being tempted to take the car and split?" My sickness only increased my concern over Jim's self-control.

Telling me not to worry, Jim took Ruth and Jackie to the emergency ward, where a doctor quickly treated our little son. As the doctor examined Jackie, Ruth noticed Jim looking into the doctor's open bag. She suspected he might be casing it for drugs. The doctor saw the needle tracks on Jim's arms, so he cautiously moved the bag away from where Jim stood. This averted any possible problem for Jim.

Jim, Ruth, and Jackie returned home, where Ruth quickly put Jackie to bed, then rushed to prepare dinner. That whole week she nursed me, served Jim regular meals, and cared for our less-than-well son. I thought she would break under the strain. Beyond all this, my aunt had flown from New York that week and was staying at our house. Jim slept on the couch and my aunt was sleeping in Jackie's room. Things could hardly have been more unnerving for my longsuffering wife.

At two o'clock one morning Jackie awoke with a temperature of 105.4 degrees. Alarmed, I forced Ruth to stay in bed, grabbed a bottle of alcohol, and began to rub our son's feverish body. As I rubbed I prayed, fighting to stay awake. Jackie made no response, but finally dozed fitfully off to sleep. About five o'clock, I became aware that his body appeared cooler. He opened his eyes feebly and looked up at me, a faint smile on his lips.

Taking his temperature again, I leaped inside with joy. The thermometer read 100 degrees! His fever had broken. I thanked God, put Jackie back in his bed, and went soundly to sleep. When I awoke I felt well enough to get back out on the street, back to work.

After breakfast Jim came to me, his head hanging low. "Vince," he said, "you know the West Palm Beach rap? I've decided what I'm going to do about it." I waited for him to go on. "I know I could get maybe five years for forgery, but I might as well get everything off my chest and out of the way."

"Are you sure you want to do this, Jim?" I asked.

His reply thrilled me. "No, it isn't what I want to do. But I've prayed about it and I feel this is what God would have me do." So that day Jim went to West Palm Beach and turned himself in to the authorities. As I feared, he was arrested and jailed pending the trial. Many letters I've received from him indicate he is still growing in the Lord. And he insists the Word of God has become very precious to him.

While in prison, Jim has been witnessing to other inmates, telling them about Jesus Christ and his wonderful love. I have tried to assure him that we are praying earnestly for God to work miraculously when his case is tried. Jim will always have a special place in my heart, for he demonstrated to me what God really can do in the life of an addict who submits himself to Jesus Christ.

6

Win Some, Lose Some

The day after Jim left us I felt empty, incomplete, as though I had lost some part of myself. Deciding to go out and see if I could find someone needing help, I tried to plan my strategy. I knew it would be easy to find a lot of people who would take advantage of any do-gooder. Many times, young persons in trouble take unfair advantage of clergymen coming into jail to see them. Thus the helper becomes the used, the vehicle by which a youth might escape from confinement. I knew this because I did it myself when I was in trouble and on drugs.

Climbing into my car, I headed toward the Broward County Jail. I wheeled into the parking lot and got out, instantly noticing a familiar figure standing in front of the jail. It was Glenn. "What are you doing here?" I asked, walking up to him.

He replied, "I don't really know, Vince. I didn't have anything more important to do, so I thought I'd come here." I told him I'd had the same feeling. While we chatted we heard someone yelling Glenn's name. Looking up at the barred jail windows, we recognized Ed, a handsome black man about twenty-three, built like an athlete.

I had met Ed on my first visit to Florida, when Denver and I visited a jail. Ed had quite a record. In fact, one judge commented that Ed had the longest federal rap sheet he had ever seen on one individual. Having access to the jails in both Dade and Broward counties, day or night, Glenn and I went up to see Ed.

After climbing up to the sixth floor, we asked the lieutenant in charge if we could see Ed. He took us to the bullpen, where Ed waited to go to trial. That day he was to face charges of possession of narcotics, grand larceny, and an indictment charging him with parole violation in New Jersey. Both Glenn and I had worked with Ed prior to this time, but neither of us had known the date of his trial.

Ed had professed to know Christ as his Savior, though his present status was uncertain to us. As he saw Glenn and me walking toward the bullpen, he said, "Man, am I ever glad to see you guys. I'm glad you remembered to come to my trial!"

"Your trial?" Glenn and I chorused together.

"Yeah! Today I'm going to trial. It's being held in the judge's chambers." We told Ed we knew nothing about it, but would try to sit through the hearing if possible. The police lieutenant told us Ed would be going to court in a few minutes and asked us to leave.

We asked Ed who the judge would be. He said his name was Judge Minnett, a former agent for the Federal Bureau of Investigation and a U.S. Commissioner. So Glenn and I went to his office and received permission from his secretary to sit in his chambers during court.

Sitting there waiting for court to begin, both Glenn and I were agreeing in prayer for Ed. After about ten minutes, in came the District Attorney followed by two U.S. Marshals, one on either side of Ed. Finally Judge Minnett entered and took his place at the head of the large conference table. We stood until he was seated.

The Court Clerk then read a statement giving the judge's name, the charge of the state against Ed, and the defendant's full name. Then the District Attorney presented facts and data about the case against Ed. Listening carefully, I thought it appeared to be an airtight case.

However, during Ed's fifteen months in prison awaiting trial, he had studied law and had written his own habeus corpus. The judge introduced this document into the record and seemed impressed by Ed's effort. As the judge looked over Ed's document, the District Attorney told the court that the state of New Jersey had already issued extradition papers signed by the Governor. The judge nodded, laid Ed's paper aside, and spoke to Glenn and me.

"And what is your role in this case? Who are you two gentlemen?" Glenn introduced himself and me, saying he was director of the House of Ichthus Coffee House in Fort Lauderdale, and I was with Turning Point Ministry, working in drug rehabilitation and education. He further told the judge that I was a minister of the gospel, that both he and I had worked with Ed.

The judge replied, "Tell me more. That's very interesting. How long have you been working with him?"

I stood and said I had recently come to the area from New York, but that Glenn had worked with Ed for nine or ten months. I said that Ed had shown a wholesome change of attitude by accepting Christ as his Lord and Savior. I told him that while in jail, Ed was motivating other young people to turn away from drugs.

The judge seemed impressed by my story, so I said, "Your Honor, I was given a break in life several years ago and, because of this break and people's concern for me, my life was completely changed. It was changed through a personal relationship with Jesus Christ."

When the judge heard me mention my conversion experience, he opened his eyes wide, smiled, and said, "Thank you very much, Reverend Guerra. Please be seated." Turning to Ed, he asked, "Do you really want to go home, son?"

Ed replied, "I sure do, your honor."

"Do you think you've learned your lesson?"

"Yes, I did and I have."

"Are you going to go straight?"

"Yes," Ed responded emphatically.

"All right," said Judge Minnett, "I'm going to place you on a ten-year probation. You've got ten years to straighten out."

"But, your honor," the District Attorney interrupted, "the extradition papers have already been signed by the state of New Jersey!"

The judge intoned, "We'll notify New Jersey as to what our action was in this case." Turning to Ed, he said, "If I catch you or hear of you getting into trouble once more, you're really going to be in for it." Ed said he was through with trouble.

The judge said he would release Ed later that day, and Glenn and I heaved a big sigh of relief. As we left the judge's chambers, the District Attorney came running over to us and said, "I don't know who you guys are or what you've got going for you. But according to legal statistics, Ed's chances of being released today—even with a ten-year probation—were one in one thousand."

Glenn and I walked over to a sheltered spot in the foyer and bowed our heads to thank God for that one small chance. How good it was to know we could be so attuned to God we could sense his leading.

But now we needed a different kind of leading from God: assurance of his help in locating a halfway house. Glenn was keeping several young men in a house loaned to him for that purpose. In fact, the owner's son was one of the boys staying there. These young men used several hallucinating drugs, but were not yet on hard dope. They lived in the house, Glenn supervising their activities and trying to guide them away from drugs.

Several of the fellows worked, and Glenn felt we should take Ed to this house, let him regain his health, and get him a job. We both knew a larger facility was desperately needed in order to give more addicts an opportunity to go straight. Guests in our rehabilitation house often are unable to work at fulltime jobs, not because they were physically weak, but because they fell under the temptation of the full week's pay.

Knowing that a fellow with seventy-five or eighty dollars found it difficult to stay straight, Glenn often took the men's paychecks and opened savings accounts for them. That way, they had a financial start when they felt ready to leave our care.

Glenn called his wife and told her Ed Scott might call around four o'clock to ask for Glenn. Barbara was to tell him that Glenn and I were speaking to a teachers' group at a school, and that he should wait at the jail for us. After the school engagement we hurried toward the jail, but got caught in downtown traffic. It was after five P.M. when we reached the jail. Ed was nowhere in sight, so we called

Barbara to ask if Ed had contacted her. She hadn't heard from him.

We asked the authorities if they knew where Ed was, and were told he had checked out around 4:30. Glenn and I were upset. I called Ruth and told her not to expect me for dinner. Glenn and I drove through the black community seeking Ed. We drove around for four or five hours, but never saw him, nor did we meet anyone who knew where he had gone.

The next couple of days I spoke in several churches and civic clubs, some of which were Jewish. I always share my story of how Jesus Christ helped me get off my drug addiction, and have learned that Jewish audiences are not offended when they hear of Christ as the helper of the needy. Becoming acquainted with many Jewish men, I've discovered them to be more open in attitude to learn about Jesus Christ than was formerly true. Many Jews I've witnessed to, have accepted Jesus as Messiah, the Savior of the world.

The day after Ed was released from jail, I spoke for the Miami Kiwanis Club. Following this, Cleve Bell and I drove to Dade County Jail for the regular encounter session. Denver Smoot met us in the jail parking lot. He appeared very tired and his steps dragged as he followed us into the jail. He normally can outwalk most men.

Near the jail entrance, I saw a black man emerge from the courthouse. I grabbed Cleve's arm and asked, "Isn't that Ed over there?" He nodded and I let out a shrill whistle. Ed looked at me and I waved to him. As he sauntered over toward us, I ran to him and said, "Where in the world were you yesterday?" He asked what I meant, so I said, "You were supposed to get in touch with us when you were released from jail."

He said, "Nobody told me to contact you. And besides, I have only Glenn's old telephone number, so I couldn't reach you." We apologized for not making plans clear to Ed and told him we had a place for him to stay until he could work and be on his own. This made him very happy.

Denver said he wanted to take Ed to Eston Hunter's office. I thought Denver didn't look well enough to do anything, and suggested that I take Ed and let Denver go into the jail. Denver repeated that he had some questions to ask Ed. I offered to go with him, but he insisted that I go with Cleve to the encounter session. I cautioned him to watch Ed closely so he wouldn't get away from us again and possibly go back on drugs.

Denver said he wouldn't let Ed out of his sight, so Cleve and I went on into the jail. We spent about thirty minutes in the encounter group when in came Denver, walking slowly, his face ashen. In a faint voice he whispered in my ear, "Vince, you better get me out of here and take me home right away." I ask him why, and he replied, "My heart." I knew he had heart trouble, so I excused myself, called Cleve to help me, and together we loaded Denver into my car. We eased him down in the back seat so he could partially recline.

Suddenly I remembered Ed. "Where is Ed, Denver?" I asked. He said Ed had to go over to the court house to see a friend. I told him he shouldn't have let Ed go alone. Although I didn't want to make an issue of it with Denver feeling ill, I thought we'd seen the last of Ed. Ed's profession of faith in Christ still left him with many ideas needing changing and upgrading. This would happen only through Bible study, Christian fellowship, and much prayer.

Like a knife slicing into my brain, the thought came that it would be so much easier to work with addicts if only we had a halfway house. Denver said Ed had promised to come to the car in ten minutes. As I waited, I earnestly prayed for Ed, for Denver, and for our still-future halfway house.

While we waited, Denver lay with his eyes closed, trying to rest and ease the chest pains he knew so well. Twenty minutes crawled past, but Ed did not come. We finally had to leave to take Denver home.

At 5:30 my telephone rang. Jamming the receiver to my ear, I was thrilled to hear Ed's soft drawl. He said he was all right and that he would be in touch with us the next evening. On Thursday night he called to say he was ready to go with us to the house where the guys were staying. Going to the address he gave us—his mother's— we got him and went to our encounter session at the House of Ichthus.

That evening I learned that Maria, the Cuban girl who wanted to go back into the ghetto area to help her friends, had gone back to using drugs. That same day, a young man, Bob Buillon, came to us from Houston, Texas. He had heard that we would find him a room, but we had filled all the rooms available to us.

Denver asked Glenn and me if we would drive Bob to a farm for alcoholics located 125 miles from Ft. Lauderdale. I asked him if the people knew Bob was coming. Denver said no, but he felt so ill he was unable to call them himself. He looked as if he were drawing from his last bit of reserve strength.

Not wanting to make things any more difficult for Denver, Glenn and I prepared to take Bob to the farm. But while still at the group encounter session, we heard Ed give a brief testimony of how God helped him in jail and while he was in court.

Poor Ed! He soon landed a job, made contact with his old crowd, and began to use drugs again. While at the halfway house, he allegedly took money from other fellows. Glenn told him that if he continued to live as he was, he'd have to leave the program.

Ed did leave, at which time Glenn told him, "Ed, you're going to be gunned down like a dog, unless you let the Lord take over your life." Ed cried, thanking everyone for our prayers and our concern for his life. I thought, *This articulate, artistic young man has so much to offer. Oh, if only he surrenders his talent for writing and poetry to God.* I felt God might use him as a journalist or even a minister, if only Ed would yield to God.

The ride to Stewart, where the farm was located, was uneventful. There we met a man named Mickey Evans, whom I had met at a drug workshop. I asked him if he would take Bob in. Mickey said he would on a temporary basis. "Good enough," I agreed, and we let Bob out and headed back toward Fort Lauderdale.

7

Vision and Provision

On our way back to Fort Lauderdale, Glenn shared some of the dreams he had concerning our need for a half-way house. I said, "Let's drive around town to see if there are any buildings for sale or rent. We've got to get something going for these addicts." We both knew that at any moment the owner of the house now in use could demand possession, and our fellows would be outside.

We saw many buildings that night, some for sale, others for rent. But finally we came to a place we had heard about: the Old Pompano Hotel. Looking at it, I tried to visualize what it might look like as our own building. I remarked to Glenn, "I feel like this is going to be ours some day."

Glenn and I sat down on the front steps of that gigantic building. Then from a sitting position we slipped to our knees and asked God for it. Like other Christian venturers before us, we claimed that property for the glory and honor of God. Just as we finished praying, a drunken woman came reeling out of the hotel and asked what we were doing. I told her we were praying and asking God for the building. She stared at us and in a thick-tongued monotone said, "Man, I thought *I* was drunk."

I said to Glenn, "Can you imagine what would happen if the police went by and saw us kneeling here, praying for this building? For sure, they would run us in for public intoxication." Maybe we were intoxicated at that, but on something far greater than 100 proof whiskey. It was the new wine of the Holy Spirit, generated by our living in tune with the great God of the universe.

Soon the newspapers learned of our work in Fort Lauderdale and Dade County. They gave us very good publicity. Socialites reading about our work invited Glenn and me to speak for various social functions. Of course, we were delighted to comply. Usually, after such engagements, a few women offered to give coffees at the House of Ichthus. This gave our Turning Point ministry good promotion in the community.

During these coffees, Barbara, Glenn, Ken Grossman— who heads up the Urban Ministry in Fort Lauderdale and I had opportunity to share what we were doing to better the entire community. From these social gatherings came a telephone answering service, donations of money, and more publicity than we dreamed possible.

All of this was very much appreciated, especially the monetary contributions. We needed many thousands of dollars to underwrite the total program. Salaries had to be paid, food and medicines provided for our houseguests, staff additions were necessary as our work expanded. We accounted for every cent people generously gave.

Weeks passed as we continued to inquire about several other buildings we learned were available. We looked further into the cost of the Old Pompano Hotel, the building for which Glenn and I had prayed. The owners wanted $95,000 for it, but the price included a liquor license, something we had no use for. Unable to get the hotel without the liquor license, we bade farewell to that idea.

It seemed things just weren't working in our favor, then one day as Glenn drove around he asked God to lead him to a good location. He kept driving until he found himself on Riverside Drive, a road along a canal in Fort Lauderdale. He pulled up beside an enormous building that appeared deserted. Glenn jumped out of the car and walked around the building. He recognized it as the annex to the city hall. It was the old city hall, but had been a rundown hotel before that. Marveling at his find, Glenn hurried to the city manager's office and inquired about the building.

The assistant city manager, Skip Johnson, told Glenn the annex was up for grabs and said we might even get it for a dollar a year. Glenn called me at once, asking me to meet him for a tour of the property. I hurried to the spot, where we went through what must have been forty-five rooms. We knew the building would need a lot of work, but felt it might house seventy or more young people. Both Glenn and I began to dream of a vision realized.

On two floors were spacious five-room apartments, one for my family and one for Glenn and Barbara, I reasoned. It seemed almost too perfect to be true. The city manager's clerk told us we would have to appear before the city commissioners' meeting on the first Monday of the month to find out the particulars on this property. That meeting was just a few days away, with no time to write a letter of intention, as we were supposed to do.

Praying earnestly, we decided to attend and take our chances on being allowed to speak to the commissioners. Denver, Glenn, and I were conspicuous in the first row of seats at that meeting. Just before the commissioners adjourned for lunch, the chairman asked if we had any item of business to present.

We hadn't even selected a spokesman, but I got the nod from the others and proceeded to explain our interest in the old annex, outlining our Turning Point ministry to young persons on drugs, our jail program, and our educational ministry in schools.

The chairman, Mayor Clement, explained that we couldn't have the building because it has been promised to Florida Atlantic University to use as a graduate school for approximately eight years. Asking if a lease had been signed, we received a negative answer. The chairman insisted that a moral obligation held them to this decision to give the building to FAU. He also said the Florida Historical Society had been given permission to restore the building to its original state, making it a landmark in Florida.

When I asked if they would please reconsider their decision, Mayor Clement said, "No, the verbal agreement has been given, and nothing can be done about that." I thanked the group for giving us time to present our request. The mayor told us to inquire at the building commissioner's office to see if other city buildings were available. He said something might be worked out.

As we started to leave, a young minister from an area church stood up and said he didn't think we had received a fair hearing. He felt our program was far more important than restoring a landmark or enlarging a university. He told the commissioners he felt they owed the young people this property.

Some of the commissioners appeared to be upset by his remarks, but we were completely dumbfounded to think we had an ally, however little weight his words might carry. When the meeting ended, the minister came to us and asked, "You are salvationists, aren't you?" We acknowledged we were. "You believe in the power of prayer, don't you?" We said we did. He continued, "Well, keep praying for these politicians, that God's love will engulf them."

Knowing that no contract had been signed, we felt we still had a chance to get the property. So we went after it, especially after learning there was no other property available from the city. The following month, Glenn and I returned to the commissioners' meeting. I felt refreshed and assured after all the Bible reading and prayer I had engaged in during the past month. It had been good discipline for me, like an athlete preparing for a special event.

Several of our young people went with us to the meeting. It must have been an unusual experience, judging from the stares we got from some of the city fathers. Early in the meeting, we were asked to speak. Mayor Clement was absent, so we presented our story to Vice-Mayor Cox. We quickly assured the commissioners that we had offers from contractors to donate time, money, and materials to remodel the building for our use.

Several of them asked us questions about our ability to keep up a building as large as this one. We tried to field each question as it came, and answered them as accurately as we could. Each of us knew there was no reason to gloss over areas of obvious weakness. If this building was intended for our use, God would see that we got it.

After the commissioners debated the matter, and we had pleaded our case as fully as we knew how, Commissioner Friesen said to Vice-Mayor Cox, "Well, let's give them the building. Florida Atlantic University doesn't really need it, nor does the Historical Society."

Mr. Cox replied, "Well, we really know nothing about this group." Quickly we told them we were endorsed by the Broward County Narcotics Guidance Council. The acting-mayor said, "If you can get Sheriff Stack to give you an okay in written form, indicating your good standing with the Broward County Narcotics Guidance Council, we'll give you the property."

After the meeting was over, we drove to the office of Sheriff Stack and obtained the written endorsement. We had been asked by the City Commission to return the following month. That month dragged by so slowly I thought it would never pass. And then at the meeting of the Commission, we were told that the building was to be given to the University and the Historical Society, after all.

All the hope we had built up collapsed like a bursted balloon. We had worked day and night to develop a plan that would make the building habitable and homelike. We had raised our expectations so high, and now they plunged dangerously toward the rocks of despair. But, in spite of our apparent defeat, we did not feel that God had abandoned us.

One day I asked Glenn if he was discouraged. He said, "No, not in the least. If anything, I'm more encouraged than ever, because now we know that Satan doesn't want us to have a facility like that." I agreed, knowing that an effective rehabilitation program with its own halfway house would thwart Satan's efforts to keep young people in the clutches of drug-induced evils.

About three days after our initial disappointment over not getting the city's building, word came that we had to vacate the house where Glenn had several boys staying. Now, things did look bleak, for we had no place to house these young men. They could only go back to the streets —and the drug life.

One evening, a young Christian man, Ray Hamel, brought Mayor Thompson, of Wilton Manors, to see Glenn and me. They drove us to an old, wooden building, obviously vacant for years. My first glance made me think that I had never seen another house that looked so run-down, filthy, raunchy, and rat infested. Human waste littered the floor. We found marijuana on the property. We were told that hippies had occupied the building before the police drove them out.

Glenn and I walked around the dingy rooms, stumbling over debris and shaking our heads. Glenn sighed, "Well, it's better than nothing." We learned that the owner had offered us its use for six months or until he sold the property, a most unsatisfactory situation, but one which we felt might help us out of a tightening bind.

Glenn and some of the young people began to shovel out the trash, scrub windows, walls, and floors, and even to paint the drab interior of the house. Within a few days the property began to look less dull and uninviting. Some kind friends installed new flooring in part of the house, donating time and material in a labor of love.

By the time Glenn and the first young men moved in, the house began to look as if it could actually become a home. Word spread that we had a halfway house, and young people began to come to us. Television gave us a big boost when Mr. Bill Brazil of WTVJ did a documentary on our program. The courts assigned to our care a number of teen-agers who were potential hardcore drug users. Acid freaks, marijuana smokers, glue sniffers—all kinds of users showed up at our front door.

At last we began to see that God had prevented our making a big mistake. If we had gotten the large hotel building, we would not have had experience enough to operate it with dozens of people living there. This way, we had ten young men in a small house, and we quickly learned how to operate most efficiently and effectively. We thanked God for overriding our shortsighted desires, and for giving us a place just big enough for our zeal-inflated abilities.

Stan Fredericks came to work with us as our male counselor, Glenn and I spearheaded the rehabilitation program, and Denver Smoot headed up the drug work in Dade County. Patsy Duggan continued to work with female drug users.

At the halfway house we soon learned that ground rules were necessary. We asked those in the rehabilitation program not to smoke, and no acid rock music was allowed. We had discovered that smoking and acid rock music, with their strong associations to drug use, often induced flashbacks in the minds of former users. We wanted nothing to hinder the progress of these young people toward complete freedom and rehabilitation.

One young man who had been in our program for several months insisted on listening to acid rock music. A former LSD user, he had a severe flashback and tried to take his own life. He grabbed a butcher knife from the kitchen and stabbed himself several times in the abdomen, puncturing his intestines and tearing two holes in his stomach.

Rushed to the hospital, he was very near death for several days. That he lived at all, seemed to us a miracle from God. He spent several weeks in the hospital, during which time many churches prayed earnestly for his recovery. Jim's recovery was remarkably swift and complete, but the experience showed us the need for extreme care in our program of Christian rehabilitation for these sensitive young people.

8

A Wild Trip--Home!

In mid-June Ruth and I packed to travel northward to an international church convention. I felt the need of spiritual refreshing and the company of Christian friends, new and old. I told a friend of mine I was going to the convention to have my spiritual batteries recharged, and I looked forward to the meeting with more than anticipation.

Ruth packed so many clothes for Jackie, herself, and me, that I feared we wouldn't get them into our car. So we asked Stan Fredericks if we could drive his car, a 1967 Chrysler Imperial. He'd just bought the car, and freely offered us the use of it. His work with the boys at the halfway house would keep him close to it while we were gone, so he wouldn't really need his car. Eagerly we packed the car and left for Columbus, Ohio, where I was to speak the following Sunday.

We worked our way out to the Florida State Parkway and had driven about forty-five miles when a tire blew out. Looking over at my wife, I announced, "Well, we're off to a flying start." I hopped out to put on the spare, only to discover there was no lug wrench in the trunk. Fortunately, in about fifteen minutes a state trooper came along, saw our plight, and stopped to let me use his lug wrench.

78

While changing tires, I casually asked the trooper if there was a drug problem in that area. He wanted to know why I asked, so I told him about my work with Turning Point ministry. He said, "Yes, we do have quite a drug problem. In fact, my seventeen-year-old brother is having flashbacks almost every night, a result of his drug use." He said his brother really wanted and needed help, but hardly knew where to turn.

By this time I had almost finished changing tires, so I asked Trooper Green if he knew Jesus Christ as his personal Savior. He responded, "No, but I know what you're driving at, and I've been thinking about it." He said his deceased parents had been splendid Christians.

I asked him, "Why don't you make your commitment to Jesus Christ, since you feel responsible for your brother's welfare? Who knows but what your decision for Christ could have a good effect on your brother, too?"

Officer Green replied, "I don't have any reason why I shouldn't. As a matter of fact, I should. But I just don't feel that I can right now." He said he did believe in God, and that he planned someday to become a Christian. I saw our conversation had ended as I handed back his lug wrench. Trooper Green saluted me, wheeled away, and climbed into his patrol car. My heart fell in dismay that he had been so near to the Kingdom, but had rejected Christ's offer.

As we drove along the Parkway, I noticed that the car was overheating. Steam boiled from under the hood. I had to pull off the highway several times to allow the radiator to cool. Ruth and I drove only about 400 miles that day—since we couldn't use the air conditioning because of the overheating problem. We stopped at a motel for the night, tired but excited about new experiences just ahead of us.

The next morning we drove to a restaurant to eat breakfast. Ruth left her purse on the front seat of the car. While we ate a delicious breakfast, someone took her purse. Upon our return to the car, Ruth noticed her purse was missing. Although there was nothing in it of great value, it was quite a loss to her. She looked at me and asked, "What next?"

I grunted, "We continue." The scenery through Tennessee was more than beautiful, it was breathtaking. The hills tied together by the highway ribbons of concrete and asphalt, the green trees and lush grass, the rainbow-colored flowers, all made us forget the blowout, the lost lug wrench, the overheated radiator, the stolen purse. We thought only of God's creation, his genius, his wonderful love.

We stopped that night in Nashville, Tennessee, where I put Jackie in the motel pool. He really enjoyed the water, kicking and splashing, his dark eyes flashing in delight. People paused to watch us play together as the sun dropped over the hills. That night was one of the most restful we had had for months. The next day we arrived in Ohio, then on to Indiana for the convention.

What I expected to be a week of spiritual retreat for me was, instead, a week of meetings, visiting a number of civic clubs, press interviews, and several speaking engagements. The highlight of the entire week, for me, came when Denver Smoot and Cleve Bell shared with thousands of persons the story of Turning Point ministry. Many people seemed to be inspired by their story of what God was doing in Florida to win lives away from the drug scene. I felt ready and eager to return to my work and our dreams of a permanent halfway house.

Eston Hunter and Cleve Bell were to accompany Ruth, Jackie, and me on the southbound ride to Florida, so I rented a U-Haul luggage carrier to fit on top of the car. This gave us more room inside. We had been on the road about twenty minutes when a tire went flat. To my dismay, I remembered that my spare had been used, and I had not had the blown out tire replaced. We borrowed a lug wrench, removed the flat tire, and took it to a service station for repair. In about two hours we were on our way again. I was glad for the company of Cleve and Eston, both of whom were great helpers.

Approaching Tennessee, we had another blow out, and had to drive on that tire until we found a service station. There we had to replace the tire with a new one, at an unbelievably high price. Driving on into the mountains of Tennessee, we blew a head gasket on the engine. This kept our speed below forty-five miles an hour, and gave me more to be concerned about, since I had borrowed the car from Stan Fredericks.

We decided not to stop to have the car repaired, thinking it might cost us an arm and a leg for repairs, to an out-of-state car. After much discussion, we decided to drive straight through to Florida, changing drivers often to keep one person from becoming too tired. After leaving the convention site around 6 A.M. Monday, we arrived in Miami on Tuesday evening around 5:30. The last twenty-four hours were extremely difficult, with all of us tired and groggy from fumes from the engine. Little Jackie became sick—all over the back seat—and this did nothing to help our situation.

One time, in my utter tiredness, I looked upward and whispered, "Why us, Lord? Why us?" Later, however, we looked back upon our whole experience and thanked God for safety. We even laughed about our problems.

My main concern was to get the car back to Stan and explain what had happened. I wouldn't blame him for being upset with me for what had happened. But on Wednesday, when I returned the Chrysler and told him all that had happened, Stan just said, "You poor people."

When I told him I knew it was going to cost quite a bit of money to have the car fixed, he told me he had just bought the car before I borrowed it, and that it had a sixty-day warranty. So everything would be repaired by the dealer who sold the car to Stan.

Stan then told me the sad story about Jim, the young man who stabbed himself in the abdomen. Jim had come to us in mid-December 1969, a confused, sick, emotionally disturbed person. After some time, Jim found a reality in Jesus Christ, accepting him as Lord and Savior. Though he had been an acid-head, Jim broke away from the drug scene and came to live at Turning Point Halfway House.

At that time we allowed young people to smoke outside the building. I had been against this from the start— knowing the trouble that could easily result from smoking plain cigarettes. Both other staffers thought it would be easier on the persons we worked with if we let them smoke outside.

It soon became obvious that smoking meant more to some of the fellows than did Bible study and personal devotions. As Glenn and Barbara and our other staff persons saw the problem become more severe, they decided to establish a rule against smoking in or around the halfway house.

It was difficult to break the news of the rule to the fellows, and some of them left the program when we told them. Jim stayed with us, however, and seemed to make good progress. He was allowed to do his own shopping, go for walks by himself, run errands for the house. He earned our complete trust. Then something happened.

Jim began to go back into the hip scene again. Since he had no money, he stole items from shopping centers. He started to smoke again. In his spare time he listened to acid rock music at the Record Shack. We knew that prior to his coming to Florida, Jim had been involved with an acid rock band—this was a major weakness for him.

One night Jim was allowed to stay in the halfway house by himself while Glenn took the other fellows out for recreation. Instead of reading his Bible, Jim began to smoke cigarettes and groove on acid rock music coming from the stereo turned up as loudly as it would play. Stimulated by the smoking and vibrating music, Jim went into a flashback, grabbed a butcherknife, and stabbed himself repeatedly.

When taken to the hospital, he was declared to be only a pint of blood away from death. Immediate surgery was performed, but Jim lingered for some days at death's door. Praying Christians were told of Jim's need, and many churches became prayer partners in his behalf. His recovery once begun, was rapid, and this was his condition when I first saw him in the hospital.

He told me about his smoking habit and his liking for rock music. He also assured me that he was finished with the hip scene and all it involved, for he realized what associating with it could mean. The Turning Point ministry staff all felt a deep burden for Jim and others like him.

About this time, Ruth shared with me the wonderful news that we were to become parents again. Although I was elated, I fretted because our non-functioning air conditioner made our house too hot for Ruth's comfort. I arranged for her and Jackie to fly home to Canada, intending to drive up later to get them, visit my family in New York, then return to Florida. Driving Ruth and Jackie to the Fort Lauderdale airport, I watched the huge jetliner thrust its way into the sky, praying that Ruth would find in Ontario needed relief from the oppressive heat.

Before Ruth left for Canada, we learned that Stan Fredericks had a cancerous growth on his lip. Since it required surgery, we wondered who would stay at the halfway house while he was in the hospital. Ruth's going to Canada for a visit allowed me to move into the vacancy left by Stan. The day he left for the hospital, staff members and guests at the halfway house gathered to pray for his successful surgery and speedy recovery and return.

Stan's operation was completely successful, and I thought I would soon get to leave for Canada to get Ruth and Jackie. But then we learned about a building that was for sale or rent. It sounded like a pretty good possibility for a permanent rehabilitation center for us, so I felt I should stay in Miami to investigate the situation closely.

I called Ruth to tell her about my need to stay in Florida. She sounded rested and said Jackie was fine. Both were as homesick to see me as I was to see them. I told her to stay in Canada as long as she wished, but after being away two weeks she was ready to come home. I arranged for her to fly. This cleared the way for me to remain in Florida to see what could be done about the building we might rent or buy for a permanent halfway house.

One of the young men at our temporary house was the son of a realtor. The father, Mr. Fred Ramos, came to see Glenn and me about the available building. He then took Glenn to see the property. Glenn was so excited he drove Barbara and me out to look at the building. As we approached it, I couldn't put into words my feeling that this was just what we had been looking for all the time.

The building was a huge, thirty-room complex located on four and one-half acres of beautifully landscaped ground. We toured the building, noting the new wall-to-wall carpeting, new air conditioners throughout—even the six-car garage was air conditioned. I took special notice of the two four-room apartments. I thought: *One for Glenn and Barbara, and one for Ruth, Jackie, the baby and me.*

Inquiring into the price of the property, we learned the owner was asking $200,000 for it. Or he would rent it for $1,500 per month, on a year-to-year lease. Any damage done would be repaired at the expense of the renter. We could only approach our Board of Trustees with the details and allow them to make the decision about the property in question. We knew that our temporary house was again about to be lost. We desperately needed more rooms, hopefully, in a place of our own.

The trustees felt they should tour the property before making a decision one way or the other. They made the tour, with much the same reaction as my own. They felt that this was the place for our Turning Point halfway house, and that we should step out by faith and take it before it was lost to us.

Glenn and I were overjoyed when we received the green light to rent the property with an option to buy. Amazingly, at the moment we took possession of the house, we had the princely sum of $300 in our general fund and around $60 in our building fund. Yet, here we were renting a building that would cost us $1,500 every month. And that sum did not include utilities. Was ours an act of faith or stupidity? We chose to believe it was the former.

By the end of the first month, one donor had contributed one thousand dollars. Many other individuals and churches and civic groups began to support our program, some making single contributions, others putting Turning Point Halfway House on a monthly support basis.

As soon as Ruth and Jackie returned from Canada, I took them up to see the apartment that would become our home. Ruth fell in love with it as quickly as I had when I first saw it. Her only question: "How soon can we move in?" brought the satisfying response: "In about one week." On August 19, 1970, Ruth, Jackie, and I moved into our new apartment in Turning Point's own halfway house.

While packing to move, I received a telephone call from a parole officer in Miami. The man, Mike Keller, told me about a young fellow who wanted to go into a halfway home. He asked me if I would come to Miami to meet Bob, a young addict from Brooklyn, New York. I told Mr. Keller I would have to interview Bob anyway to see if he was ready to enter our program, and we made an appointment for the three of us to meet.

As I drove to Dade County Jail in Miami, I recalled that in that jail very recently a minister's young son had been strangled to death by other inmates. I thought remorsefully about the wages of sin, about its awful consequences to a victim and his family and friends. I hoped to be able to help young Bob—provided he wanted to be helped.

While waiting for Bob to come to the interviewing room, I learned that Ed was in that jail, and asked if we could see him. Permission was granted and, as Ed walked in, we noticed he had a bad limp. Glenn, who was with me that day, asked Ed what had happened. Ed replied that he had been in a rundown, abandoned theater, getting ready to use some dope, when the police pulled a raid on the hang-out.

Ed—knowing he had broken his probation terms, for which he could be imprisoned for ten years—decided to run for it. An officer yelled for him to stop. He didn't, and the officer fired several shots, a couple of them hitting Ed in the leg. Ed said he lay on the sidewalk, blood streaming from his wounds, and thought of Glenn's words: "If you leave our program, you're going to be gunned down like a dog."

As Glenn, Mike Keller, and I were called to the interviewing room to see Bob, I couldn't help thinking how true Glenn's warning to Ed had been. Then we had to give our attention to young Bob. His story was that he had started using drugs when he was sixteen years old. He had been arrested on several charges ranging from possession of narcotics to grand larceny. To my questions Bob gave very short answers. This disturbed me a bit.

For the most part he responded with a short, Yes, No, or, Maybe. When I asked him if he wanted to come into a program such as ours, he couldn't give me a direct answer. I asked him if he wanted to come to Turning Point in order to stay out of jail, and he said, "No." But he didn't give any reason or explanation. The interview took only a few minutes, due to the interviewee's attitude of apparent indifference. Mike Keller agreed that Bob's attitude was rather cold, but said, "Bob wasn't like this when I talked with him before."

As we were leaving the cell area, Ed called to us, "I'm sorry. If I ever get out of this mess, I want to come back into your program." We assured him that if he got off without prison time, he could come back into our program, perhaps picking up where he left off. Or, we told him, if he did serve a prison term, his place would be waiting for him when he was released.

Outside the building, Mike asked me what I thought about Bob's chances in our program. I looked at him and said, "Sorry, Mike, but I don't think he'd be good for the program."

"But will you take him anyway?" Mike almost pleaded. "Will you do me this favor, Vince, against your better judgment?"

Reluctantly, I replied, "This is against my better judgment, but—okay, we'll accept him."

The next day I had to pick up Bob and bring him back to our halfway house. I watched him closely for a few days, but saw nothing to justify my suspicions of him. Bob showed himself to be a good worker and an asset to our program. He was willing to cooperate with us in every way. He was very helpful to me during our move into the halfway house. He seemed to know just what to do and how to do it.

Bob Alnieri, a Christian businessman who runs a dry-cleaning operation loaned us a van-type truck so we could move. Bob and I made several trips to move all our belongings from Hollywood to Pompano Beach, where our new halfway house is located. I found his help was invaluable.

The weekend after my family moved into the halfway house, I flew to Dallas, Texas, to speak before a large youth convention. I left Fort Lauderdale airport at 7 A.M., with Glenn and Barbara, Ruth and Jackie to see me off. Just before boarding the plane, I joined them in a prayer for God's blessing on the halfway house and upon my efforts to minister to youths at the Dallas convention.

The convention was in its second day when I arrived in Dallas. Immediately I learned of some minor disturbances the previous night. Some persons said there were protests against the contemporary mood of the program. Others thought the protest was planned. Still others said it was valid. I felt butterflies begin to flutter in my midsection.

Those butterflies stampeded—or rioted—when I learned that before I would speak that night, several well-known athletes would share their Christian testimonies. Among those who would share were Carroll Dale, Bart Starr, and Bill Glass, greats among the ranks of professional football players. I thought, *With names like those, why am I here?* But I was convinced God had a purpose I could fulfill.

In my motel room before the meeting that night, I tried to marshall my rampaging thoughts. I wondered if great evangelists ever were bothered by the jitters. I wondered how things were going back at the halfway house in Pompano Beach. I wondered how Ruth was doing in her yet-unfamiliar surroundings. Was Jackie getting into trouble, or getting lost in the huge building? Did I really expect to speak to five thousand young people and their counselors, with superb athletes much more in demand? Still, I prayed that God would use me to do whatever he wanted me to do. I prayed that I would be sensitive and aware of his presence.

At the convention hall, I was directed to a dressing room at the back of the stage area. Entering the room, I immediately saw Bart Starr, Carroll Dale, and Mike Mc-Gee, all members of the Green Bay Packers. I presented them with copies of my first book, *The Turning Point*. A few minutes later, Bill Glass came in and I had the thrill of meeting him and presenting him with a copy of my book. I consider Mr. Glass an outstanding evangelist.

We received the nod that it was time for the service to begin and walked out onto the gigantic stage. I saw a number of pastors and adult counselors from Florida, seated there with their young people from several churches where I had spoken. One minister, Pastor Don Pickett, came over and told me the group was praying for me. What a boost this gave my wavering self-confidence! Also, I knew that Ruth, Glenn, and many others back home were praying.

The great audience broke into some of the most inspiring singing I have ever heard. It was spirited, yet reverent; contemporary, yet timeless, the message of God's love told in youthful melodies. I was lifted in an experience of worship from the first note. Then the athletes were introduced, after which each gave a brief testimony. They received a thunderous ovation from the appreciative crowd. In all, some forty minutes expired before I was ready to speak. I thought, *Man, these people must be tired of sitting here. I'd better cut my talk short, and make it good.*

When chairman Ken Prunty introduced me, I thought people looked at each other with a Who's-Vince-Guerra? look in their eyes. As I stepped to the rostrum, Dr. T. Franklin Miller, president of Warner Press, came forward and presented me with a splendidly bound copy of my own book. I could only gulp for a minute, then I was alone, and it was time to speak.

As I introduced my topic, I noticed people running in and out near the sides of the convention hall. A sudden rain had caused people to dash madly to roll up windows —and ruined my introduction. Raising my voice to compensate for the confusion, I felt my throat give way and could only talk at low volume. As my voice receded, the amplifier quit working. I thought I had just about finished before getting started.

Then Ken Prunty was at my side, fastening a neck microphone cord around me, his voice low and reassuring, "Hang in there, Vince." Momentarily I dropped my head and prayed silently. I felt a release, and began to speak. Noise stopped. People became still as they listened to stories of the power of Christ to redeem, transform, renew the lives of drug addicts. There was an awe in the entire building, and I knew it was not my doing. It had to be from God.

At the conclusion, an opportunity was given for those who wished to accept Christ as Lord and Savior to come forward in a public act of dedication. Twenty or thirty responded. I wondered at the slight response, until I remembered this was a church youth convention, not a group of spiritual dropouts or sophisticated heathen.

Still, I felt there should be an appropriate response by many more young persons and adults. So I asked those who wished to dedicate their lives—fully—to serve **God** in whatever way he chose, to come forward in a public witness to that affirmation. About a hundred made the first response, then dozens began streaming down the aisles from all directions, until, some later estimated, nearly thirteen hundred stood there with heads bowed as I led them in a prayer of commitment.

As the service ended, I was asked to go into the back room to see a young man who needed help. In the counseling room I met the young man, who said, "Just about everything you said tonight applies to my life. I came from a broken home. I've gone to drugs. I need help."

I told him that anyone who is lonely, despondent, insecure, being hassled by friends or family, can have power and assurance to overcome everything through complete trust in Jesus Christ. The young fellow acknowledged his need of Christ, and soon prayed to receive him. He left obviously relieved and happy. That one experience gave me as much satisfaction as did the sight of the hundreds standing in front of the stage minutes before.

The next day I was near the book tables with their display of relevant books for youths. Occasionally I autographed a book for a young person who bought a copy of *The Turning Point*. At other times I talked with new, young acquaintances. I almost broke up laughing when one smallish fellow tried to get his friends to buy copies of my book. He said in a decided drawl, "It's so-o-o inspirin'."

From that high point in Dallas, I left for an even higher point in Indiana—and a meeting with Art Linkletter.

9

The Inimitable Art Linkletter

My publisher, Warner Press, invited me to attend the state fair in Indianapolis, Indiana, where I hoped I might be able to meet Art Linkletter. Mr. Linkletter had been kind enough to write the Foreword to my first book, *The Turning Point,* although we had not met prior to his doing so. Because he believes so strongly that young people need to be helped to stay away—or to get away—from the drug problem, he graciously endorsed my book.

So I jetted from Dallas to Indianapolis, then by car to Anderson, where Warner Press is located. After an evening with friends in the editorial and sales divisions of the company, I spent a restful night at the Holiday Inn, them accompanied Warner Press personnel to Indianapolis.

Inside the huge Manufacturers' building, where exhibits were set up close together like shops in a Chinese market, I spent several hours at the Warner Press booth. The state fair is one of Indiana's greatest annual events, second only perhaps, to the famed Indianapolis 500-mile race. Thousands of people passed our booth, circulating slowly throughout the building, like sea water in a lagoon eddying slowly among pilings supporting a pier.

As I observed the activity, I noticed that not far from our booth was one belonging to the Ba'Hai faith. Casually walking over to see their literature, I noticed a young woman alone in the booth. She wore sunglasses although we were indoors, and her dark hair hung straight down her back. I asked her if she were an adherent of the faith and she acknowledged that she was. I asked her what made her become a Ba'Hai.

She slowly responded, "Well, I was lonely, with very few friends. I was searching for companions when I met some Ba'Hai people. They took me under their wings, so I just decided to become one of them."

I asked her if her newfound association had ever been a really spiritual experience. She said she didn't exactly know what I meant, so I asked her, "Did you become a Ba'Hai only because you found a kind of fellowship with them?"

She replied, "Yes, that's exactly how it was."

I told the young woman about my own lonely younger life, about my drug addiction, and about the wonderful relationship with Jesus Christ I had discovered. I told her that Christ is a splendid companion for lonely persons, that he wanted to be her friend.

As I talked, her eyes opened wider and wider, her interest became more intense. I felt that she was really receptive to my witness for Jesus Christ. Other people came up to her booth then, and I had to conclude our conversation by saying, "If at any time you become lonely, if you ever need strength, just call upon Jesus Christ. He will come to you and comfort you. He will be your dearest friend." I urged her to read the Gospel of John in the New Testament, then returned to my booth. Although disappointed that she had not given her life to Christ, I realized the truth of the Bible verse which indicates that "some sow the seed, and others reap."

I often pray for that young girl, and many others like her, who are lonely, and seeking for something to satisfy deep longings. Often they find only cheap substitutes for the real answer to life's needs. How much they need the friendship of Jesus Christ and the fellowship of God's people.

We learned that Art Linkletter would not be at the fair until that afternoon. My plane would leave Weir Cook Airport at three o'clock. One of the Warner Press salesmen, Jim Shell, said, "Let's go over to the capitol building and see if we can have a word with Art Linkletter." Mr. Linkletter, scheduled to be the chief personality attraction at the fair that day, was in town for just a few hours. He was meeting at that moment with state officials in the capitol.

When we parked the car, I said to Jim, "Let's just leave it in Christ's hands. If we're to meet Mr. Linkletter, well and good. If not, let's give thanks anyway." We bowed our heads and asked Christ to lead and direct us in this experience.

Going into the rotunda of the building, we saw many news reporters and television cameramen, all waiting to see Mr. Linkletter and Governor Whitcomb of Indiana. They were expected to appear momentarily.

While we waited for Mr. Linkletter's appearance, I noticed some hippies standing off to one side causing a bit of disturbance, I walked over to one who seemed to be a leader. He wore beads, fringe, and sandals, his hair was tangled and long. I said, "Peace, brother," and we shook hands. I asked him what was happening.

He said, "Linkletter is going around telling all the kids in high schools that if you smoke marijuana you're going to become a junkie and all that sort of stuff. What's he trying to do, use scare tactics on the kids?" He sounded pretty agitated.

"No," I replied, "I don't think he's trying to use scare tactics. I think he's trying to inform kids that their chances of addiction are much greater after using marijuana than if they'd never used it."

The guy glared at me and said, "How do you know?"

"Because I smoked it and became an addict," I said, looking him squarely in the eyes. He stared back at me and slowly smiled, then he and his friends quietly left the building.

Jim went to one of the reporters and showed him a copy of my book, *The Turning Point,* on the cover of which are the words, "Foreword by Art Linkletter." The reporter said it would be all right for me to go over to Mr. Linkletter, shake hands with him, and present him a personally-autographed copy of the book. About fifteen minutes passed, then a group of officials emerged from a side room. I saw Governor Whitcomb, then the smiling, familiar face of Mr. Linkletter.

Walking over to him, I held out the book. He looked at it, paused and said, "Hey, I have one of those books."

I said, "Yes. I'm the author of this book."

Mr. Linkletter grabbed my hand and said, "Hey, Vince, it's just great to meet you!" We talked for a few minutes as television cameras ground away and reporters scribbled furiously. Then I presented him with the personally-autographed copy of my book. I also had with me the specially-bound copy Dr. Miller had given to me in Dallas. Inside the cover Mr. Linkletter wrote, "To my good friend Vince. May God bless you in your work. Your friend, Art Linkletter."

As Mr. Linkletter spoke to the crowd there at the Capitol, he introduced me as an ex-addict who kicked the habit through Jesus Christ. He emphasized the fact that I became cured through a conversion experience with Christ, and that Christ is the "turning point" in my life. I was really inspired by the way that man spoke his convictions before the crowd.

After Mr. Linkletter finished talking to the crowd, a number of young persons asked questions. One young man read statistics compiled by some agency on the values of legalizing marijuana. Mr. Linkletter handled himself diplomatically, lovingly, yet he firmly stated that an individual can become a sociological misfit—if not a drug addict—by using marijuana. When the meeting ended, Mr. Linkletter and I had a few moments together. I wished him success and Godspeed, and he assured me he would remember me and the Turning Point ministry in his prayers.

Just as Jim Shell and I were about to leave the capitol building, a group of young people stopped us and asked me if I would accept an invitation to speak at their high school. I handed one of them a business card, telling them to contact me at my Turning Point address. It always excites me to see how interested young people are in knowing the facts about drug abuse.

Following a leisurely meal at the airport restaurant, Jim and I bade each other farewell, and I again took to the skies, homeward bound. What memories I had to share with Ruth and Jackie, with Glenn and Barbara, with Denver and Mrs. Smoot. I was ready for the plane to land at Fort Lauderdale even before it took off.

Seated in the plane beside me was a man who appeared to be in his mid-thirties. He tried to peer over my shoulder to see what I was reading as we taxied out to the runway. The book was a religious classic, *Deeper Experiences of Famous Christians,* by James Gilchrist Lawson. As the plane climbed steeply into the air, I settled back to read for a few hours. The No Smoking light went out, and the man beside me lit a cigarette and ordered a double scotch from the stewardess.

He continued to try to see what I was reading, so I turned the book slightly to give him a good view of the Scripture verses quoted in the pages I had turned to. From Isaiah 5:11-12, the words read, "Woe unto them that rise up early in the morning, that they may follow strong drink; that continue until night till wine inflame them! And the harp, and the viol, the tabret, and pipe, and wine, are in their feasts: but they regard not the work of the Lord, neither consider the operation of his hands." As he caught the meaning of what I was reading, the man looked sharply at me, suddenly coughed as if he had emphysema, and changed seats. I had to chuckle over the matter, and later when I went back to the lavatory, I passed the man. He ignored me deliberately, so I assumed the verses had hit him squarely.

Back home again in Pompano Beach, I spent long hours relating my fantastic experiences in Dallas and Indianapolis, especially my meeting with Art Linkletter. Jackie did his best to tell me his experiences, but his childish language was completely unintelligible to me. Ruth was full of news about the halfway house and events that had occurred during my seven days absence.

Plunging quickly into the work, I found myself becoming very possessive about the total program. It wasn't easy for me to admit that I thought of it as *my* program, *my* halfway house. I knew that a man can easily become a dictator in such a setting, but never thought it could happen to me. I know now that it is entirely possible, and came very close to being true. I had to turn over everything—the building, the staff members, my wife, my son—to God. He was going to have to run things, if we ever hoped to succeed.

Glenn and Barbara Bondurant live on the first floor—the girls' floor—in their own four-room apartment. Ruth, Jackie, and I live upstairs on the men's floor. We emphasized to the residents that the center is not only a place of lodging, but it is our home, to be treated with respect and care.

Many residents come to us straight from jail. Others have been living on the streets for months, sometimes years, and their manners leave much to be desired. We have to work with them just to teach them how to properly use a knife and fork at the table. Many young persons who come to us are lazy, have no desire to work. Some try to sleep with their clothes on at night, or on top of the covers so they won't have to make their beds in the morning.

Many of our residents have deep-rooted problems, not the only one of which is drugs. Sometimes I feel that drugs are only symptomatic of deeper needs. There is a restlessness within their souls, a spiritual hunger which no drug or trip can fill. That aching void is God-shaped, and a loving, redeeming, forgiving Christ can remove the ache by filling that void.

Attempts at helping these young people to respect the property of others is centered around the biblical concept of the dignity and worth of the individual. One who does not respect the property of others, really does not respect himself. We teach self-respect and respect for others by helping residents dig into the Word of God in systematic, tutored Bible study. This gives them a solid basis for their just-awakened knowledge of *who* they are and *whose* they are.

Many of these young people become interested in knowing the God spoken of in and who speaks through the Bible. Both Glenn and I believe that it is a great thrill to lead a young hippie to new life in Christ. Then we see them turn on to real life, without drugs or other artificial or superficial stimulants or depressants. It is exciting to see these young Christians begin to apply the teachings of Jesus Christ in their contemporary situation.

Our emphasis at Turning Point is for the individual to live a holy life. We urge residents to break all ties with the hip philosophy. Any young man coming to Turning Point is asked not to wear beads or other symbols. His hair must be cut a decent length, and he must give up smoking cigarettes.

Our hope is that these young persons will develop a very intimate relationship with Jesus Christ. Unless they do so while they are with us, they might easily go right back into their old environment upon their release from Turning Point. It is a truism that we tend to become like our environment. If we associate with liars, we find it easy to lie. If we associate with thieves, it becomes easy for us to steal.

We try to impress upon residents in our program their need of knowledge of the Bible, the fantastic potential offered through prayer, the depth of relationship with God made possible through Jesus Christ and the Holy Spirit. As one person put it, "Other programs try to get the person hooked on himself. But you're trying to get these young people hooked—on God!" He couldn't have been more right.

One lesson it took me years to learn is that man is not the master of all things. Evidence? Through men have come wars, pollution, sickness, evil, death. When counseling youths, we sometimes say, "You've tried your own way for fourteen, nineteen, or possibly twenty-two years. You've done what you wanted to do and have only failed. Now try God's way. You've seen what it's like on your side of the fence, now come over to God's side and try his way."

I never tell a young person the way of Christ will be easy. I say it's going to be difficult, hard to do the right thing. I can speak with absolute certainty as a result of my own experience.

Life is always exciting at Turning Point. On one occasion, I had preached for a pastor who was away from his church in Fort Lauderdale. I spoke on the subject, "After Death, What?" When I concluded the message, a young man named Tom accepted Christ as his Savior. Then his fiancee also received Jesus Christ. When Tom went home, he told his brother Bob what had happened. Bob noticed the drastic change in Tom—change for the good. Tom's witness was instrumental in getting Bob, his hardcore, heroin-addict brother, to come to Turning Point Halfway House. When he came for interview, Bob seemed familiar to Glenn. Suddenly Glenn realized that he had counseled with Bob once before, but Bob had been unwilling to really seek help.

Bob expressed amazement that we had such a place as Turning Point Halfway House, and he told Glenn and me, "You people are really sincere in wanting to help young people get off drugs." Bob readily agreed to come into our program if we would let him. We did, of course, and before a week passed he was asking questions about a Christian experience. He wanted to know how to become a Christian.

I remember well that evening as Bob and I sat outside on our lawn enjoying the last rays of sun as it dipped toward the western horizon. Sensing Bob's spiritual receptivity, I shared four Bible verses with him, after which Bob invited Christ into his heart and life. Almost immediately Bob let his mother know that he had become a Christian. She seemed so happy that both of her sons had given their lives to the Lord.

One Sunday morning just after the service ended, I stood talking with Mrs. White and her two now-Christian sons, Tom and Bob. A woman in that church walked up to Mrs. White, introduced herself, and asked her, "Are you saved?"

Mrs. White looked at me in embarrassment, then replied to her questioner, "Well, I don't know what you mean by that." Realizing she was serious, I made an appointment for Mrs. White to come to my office at Turning Point Halfway House. She gladly came to talk with me and soon we were discussing matters of a spiritual nature.

I talked with her about the meaning of salvation, the new birth experience, and we discussed the meaning of living a Christian life. Carefully I shared with her such Scripture verses as Romans 3:23, John 1:12, and Revelation 3:20. I asked her if she were sure she was a Christian. Her reply was, "No, I'm not sure, I can't say for certain that I am and that if I were to die I'd go to heaven."

"Mrs. White," I urged gently, "Instead of walking out of this office with doubt in your mind, why not make a definite commitment to Jesus Christ?"

She said very simply, "All right." Together we prayed and Mrs. White accepted Christ. Now three members of that family had become Christians within just a few days. I marvelled at the mysterious ways God works. And as the new Mrs. White left my office, I thought, *Turning Point is not just for reaching addicts. Turning Point is a center for evangelism—for all persons!*

10

The Grandma Squad

Mrs. Sweeny was a neighborhood woman who worked and served in so many wonderful ways for the Turning Point ministry. She was instrumental in seeing that we had adequate supplies of food, and she was always on the alert to help us raise finances for our growing operation. Then, in the midst of her tireless efforts to help us, Mrs. Sweeny learned she had a malignancy in one leg. Amputation was necessary.

While in the hospital convalescing from her surgery, Mrs. Sweeney was concerned primarily about one thing: getting out of the hospital in time to give a Christmas party for the residents of Turning Point Halfway House. She seemed totally unconcerned about her own condition, but always cared for the welfare of others. I thank God for giving us such friends as Mrs. Sweeney, for she was an example of a saint in shoe leather. Then, a few weeks before Christmas, Mrs. Sweeny departed this life to be with her Lord, her walk of faith at last becoming a walk of reality.

Her funeral service was not a time of mourning. It was more like a homecoming, with more smiles than sorrow noted on the faces of family members and her many friends. Certainly she was missed by loved ones, but her life had been lived to the full, and Christian friends knew her faith in Christ was an eternal faith—one that never dies.

Because of the inspiration of Mrs. Sweeny, a group of women from a local church began to help us raise funds for Turning Point. They were so active in helping to discover new sources of supplies and money, and were so consistent in coming to our halfway house to assist staff members, that we nicknamed them the "Grandma Squad." Often, when one of our resident fellows saw their cars turn into our driveway, he would yell, "Here comes the Grandma Squad!" This always brought roars of laughter from other residents, but all of them deeply appreciated the work done by these faithful women.

Many other persons, like those women, are finding ways to help in this ministry to younger members of society. Through this teamwork effort the ministry of Turning Point is strengthened and broadened. Through it we attempt to reach young women like Maria.

Maria was the young Mexican girl I had worked with earlier. When I arrived home from my Dallas and Indianapolis jaunt, Maria had just come to the halfway house for help. A heroin user, she had tried to quit, but turned instead to LSD. Now her mind was affected. In our earlier counseling with her, Maria had made a profession of faith in Christ, but had gone back into her old environment and to drug use.

Now she was extremely fearful, with a paranoid suspicion and distrust of everyone who tried to work with her. About two days after she came back to our program, Maria went into a flashback. One of the other residents came running to tell me. Hurrying to where Maria was, I grasped her hand tightly and talked her back to reality. Then I began to counsel her about her need of spiritual help. She interrupted over and over, saying something that sounded like, "All those guys! All those guys!"

Maria gradually told me her story. Deep into the drug habit, she needed more money than was available, and had turned to prostitution. Now her sense of guilt weighed heavily upon her mind. Her momentary lapses of memory while under the influence of drugs no longer gave her even a brief respite. I knew that one of three things would happen: Maria would go back on drugs; she would end up in a mental institution; she would allow Christ to effect the complete change she so desperately needed.

I asked her, "Maria, didn't you accept Christ? Haven't you recommitted your life to him?"

"Yes, I have," she replied.

"Well," I continued, "In the Lord's eyes you are pure and clean and whole again. You no longer have to think about the things you have done. Let me explain it this way. Satan is working on you by reminding you of all the sins you have committed in the past."

Thinking hard about how to explain this whole matter to her, I held out my arm. "See this scar," I said, pointing to a healed-over stab wound I'd received years ago. "When I received that wound, it bled a lot and was very sore and tender. Your mind is just that way now. But in time my wound healed, first by forming a scab, then finally a scar. Though there is a scar, yet the wound is completely healed. So with God's help, your mind will heal and you'll be completely well again."

I tried to impress upon Maria that God wanted to heal her mind, and that he would do so as she allowed him to work in her life. When I asked her if she understood, she replied. "Yes, I dig that. I can really dig it." Then she asked if I thought she would ever stop feeling guilty. I told her that if she loved Christ with her whole being and would continue to love him always, she would be rid of her feeling of guilt.

Maria became involved in the Bible studies we had for residents of Turning Point. She appeared to be growing spiritually, and became very friendly with another girl. One night the other girl announced she was leaving the program. Maria became deeply upset, went into a state of mental depression, and slashed her wrists with a razor blade.

One of our girl residents found Maria lying in the bathroom, a pool of blood around her. We rushed the unconscious girl to the hospital, where a doctor sewed up her wounds. When Maria came back to the Halfway House, she was extremely remorseful. Over and over she asked our forgiveness. Each of the staff workers prayed often with her assuring her of God's love and ours. Gradually she recovered from her depression and assumed a normal role among our residents. Because of her progress, Maria eventually was allowed to go home to her parents.

Often, as I consider the near-fatal tragedy of Maria's life, I think it is easier to work with even a heroin user than it is to help a speed freak or acid user (LSD addict), because the LSD user is so unpredictable. Even they do not know what move they will make the next moment.

One morning in my stack of mail was a letter from Jim. Eager to read what he had to say, I tore open the envelope. Here is what I read:

Vince, dig it! The time has come: the lines of the struggle which has been forming over the last thousand years are now clearly drawn and defined. We are now involved in the battle that Christ predicted. Christ's values and principles reflected through us, against society's false suggestions and moral imperatives and our increasing repression of natural conscience. You're involved, and I want to be, too.

My heart goes out to you and others like you who are fighting to save young people caught up in the belief of euphoric salvation. Too many become involved in our society's great escape policy—that God is dead—hence everything is allowable. These are the great factors that have diseased our generation and played a dominant role in molding our basic natures and inclinations.

So when we become young men we are inclined to accept and rely upon our own intelligence to deliver us. (Boy, is that vanity!) Because the more we rely on our own methods, the quicker we rush toward the very disaster we try to avert. The call is out for every person who has been gripped by Christ to involve himself. I am counting myself in with God's help. The drug problem has risen 2100% in West Palm Beach and still rising. These are towering odds, but the Lord is consistent and defeat is not in his dictionary—can you dig it?

James

P.S. Your book went over great in here. It really flipped these cats out! They think you are *to-geth-er!!* Tell everyone to hold their mud and keep the faith! May Christ come soon!!

On several occasions I visited Jim in a Florida jail, and he told me about his witnessing to many fellow inmates. He said that a small revival was breaking out in the jail. But then the guards became provoked, apparently because of the spiritual fervor they noted among the inmates. Be-

108

cause of Jim's involvement in the revival, he was placed in solitary confinement. For sixty days he lived on peas, carrots, and water.

As I talked with Jim I asked him if he wanted to come into our program when he was released from prison. When he had lived with Ruth and me in Hollywood, we had not yet obtained a halfway house, but Jim often said he wanted to get into a rehabilitation program. He now repeated his past wish to be involved in a halfway house program.

Since he was then under pre-sentence investigation, I went to see his parole officer, a Mr. Damon. I told the officer about Jim's response to my earlier working with him, and that he had been concerned about his spiritual needs. Mr. Damon seemed hard on the surface, but underneath was a fair and sympathetic man, I believed. He said, "How do I know it's not just jailhouse religion?" I tried to assure him that Jim had been leading men to Christ right in the jail. He wrote down a lot of notes then said Jim would go to court around November 13. He promised to get in touch with me so I could be present.

I went back to see Jim, telling him what Mr. Damon had told me about Jim's court appearance before Judge MacIntosh, a fair, very conservative, very stern man, I had been told. However, we trusted God to work out the details of Jim's life. I left Jim in a highly optimistic frame of mind. He seemed to feel the same way.

Two weeks later I received word that Jim had been taken from his cell to appear before Judge MacIntosh. He had been sentenced to one year in prison. I was very annoyed by this news, feeling the probation-parole officer had let both Jim and me down. There was nothing I could do to get Jim released, since he had already been sentenced.

One day as I worked in my office, a minister-friend, Fenton Moorehead, minister of the Communications Gap program and associate of Jess Moody at First Baptist Church in West Palm Beach, called me. Fenton and I had worked together with the Bondurants at the Hollywood Rock Festival. He told me he had an appointment to see Judge MacIntosh and wanted to know if I would like to go with him. He thought the judge might like to hear about our drug work at Turning Point.

I jumped at the chance and on Thursday, Fenton and I, accompanied by my wife Ruth, went to see Judge MacIntosh. During our talk, I explained our program of rehabilitation. The judge appeared to be quite impressed with our operation. Then I told him about Jim and the way I had worked with him. I told him about the mixup in dates for Jim's trial. Judge MacIntosh wrote down Jim's name, saying he would look further into the case. How thankful I was that day for friends like Fenton Moorehead.

Soon after that, I wrote Jim a letter, explaining that we had not forgotten him, that we were still working on his case. His response indicated he thought I was just another big-mouthed Christian who wasn't going to back up what I said I would do. Jim's life had been a long story of people who went just so far with him, but then gave up and let him fall flat. At this point in his life, Jim felt God was to blame for his predicament, and he had declared war upon God.

I called the judge's office several times to inquire about Jim's case. Then one day the judge's secretary called me to say Jim's case was coming up for possible mitigation. His sentence might be lightened or even lifted, depending upon the outcome of the hearing.

The day of the hearing I went to the courthouse. As I walked down the corridor, I saw Jim sitting on a bench, a cigarette dangling from his lips. He looked up at me and said drily, "What are you doing here, man?" I told him he was going before the judge for mitigation, but he didn't seem to know what I meant.

I said, "Why, Jim, you might get out of jail today." Poor Jim was so full of distrust by this time he didn't know whether to believe me or not. Then we were called into the judge's chambers.

The District Attorney asked Jim some pointed questions which Jim answered as best he could. Then the attorney asked me about the percentage of persons who are rehabilitated but return to drug use. He asked about our program, and about the number of persons we had helped. I told him and the judge that the newness of Turning Point Halfway House made detailed statistics impossible, but I explained about the great number of young persons helped through our coffeehouses and the total Turning Point ministry.

Finally the judge looked sternly at Jim and asked, "Is this what you want? Do you want Turning Point?"

Jim looked first at his lawyer, then at the judge, and replied, "Yes sir, it is."

"Are you sure?" pressed the judge.

"Yes, your Honor," Jim responded, but I could sense some reluctance on his part, as if he were not sure of himself now.

The judge finally spoke, "I probation you to three years, sixteen months of which you are to be in the Turning Point program." All during that hearing I had prayed silently for Jim, and now I watched the Lord open what had been locked and barred doors. I witnessed a miracle, just as it had been when the Apostle Peter was released from jail.

Yet, after the hearing, Jim had an unhappy attitude, and the tone of his voice was not pleasing. He seemed ill at ease. I asked him what was the matter. He grumbled, "Man, I got three years probation!"

I said, "Yes, but you're out of jail, Jim, and sixteen months will be spent in the program." I watched his reaction, then said, "Listen, if you don't want to go into the program now, you'd better go back into that courtroom and tell the judge you want to finish your time. Just forget about coming into the program!"

Hastily Jim protested, "No, no. I'll go through with the program." When we arrived at the halfway house, everyone was glad to see Jim. They had heard so much about him and expected to see a spiritual dynamo. Instead, they saw only an ex-convict without a testimony. Of course, I was quite upset by the whole situation. A number of persons earnestly began to pray for Jim. Maria, the young Mexican girl, had been corresponding with Jim during his confinement. She had had high hopes that his life would inspire her own faith and encourage her to grow in the Lord. Maria's hopes, too, were dashed.

All that day Jim was sullen, hard to communicate with. That evening I took him into my office and asked him if he wanted to go back to jail. I told him I had only to call Judge MacIntosh and back he'd go. I realized that he had only eight or nine months remaining of his original sentence. Jim was wrought up as he exploded, "Vince, do you realize that I have three year's probation?"

I replied, "So what does that mean if you're going straight? Even if you got ten years' probation it shouldn't mean anything if you really plan to go straight."

Jim stared at the floor for a long time, then said, "Yeah, go straight for what?" I told him that he had a whole life ahead of him, that he was young and had quite a future ahead—if he wanted it. He replied that he had started to conform to the prison way of life again, that he was content with lawbreaking, that he didn't want Christianity. He blurted out in anguish, bitterness, and with all the pent-up hostility of his soul, "I hate God! I've thought about doing the highest act against God and his commandments—take my own life. Man cannot reveal his hatred of God more than to take his own life." His ravings now were like an enraged animal.

Glenn Bondurant and I looked at each other, not wanting to believe we were hearing these words come from a man with the potential Jim had. I told Jim he had better watch his step because he was treading on dangerous ground. My heart felt heavier and heavier as Jim vented his anger and frustration. I remembered another young man who had come to our program just a few days earlier.

We had sensed that Morey, the other fellow, had an uncooperative attitude about him when we got him released from jail. And soon after coming to Turning Point he had managed to smuggle in some marijuana and smoked it. We soon caught on to his game and dismissed him from the program. Now I asked Jim if he wanted to go back to jail. Again he said no, that he'd stick with us for the entire program. However, his attitude did not improve. If anything, it deteriorated.

I prayed earnestly for Jim, and often prayed with him, but he seemed unable to know what he really wanted. One day I asked him, "Jim, why is there so much doubt and uncertainty in your life?" He repeated his earlier story about life in several foster homes, and of his many experiences in reformatories.

He said, "Every home I went to, the people were nice to me the first three or four weeks. But then the car from the orphanage would come to get me and take me away because the people had gotten disgusted with me and didn't want me anymore." Then he began to share what was eating at him deep inside. "When you didn't come to my trial I figured you were just like all the other people I've known.

I told him the trial was held without our knowledge, to which he replied he already knew that. I finally said, "Why don't you just give God a chance in your life? You were being used by him in jail and won a lot of fellows to the Lord. You've influenced lives. Why don't you slow down long enough so you can catch up with yourself and listen to what God has to say to you." Jim began to cry, and my heart went out to him. He seemed crushed. After we prayed, Jim walked out and for the next few days appeared to be in a better mood.

Gradually Jim began to talk more freely with other residents, although he was standoffish with others. One day he came into the office where Glenn and I were talking and asked, "Can I tell you guys something? I don't know why, but God has his hand on me and he doesn't want to let me go." Then he told us about Bruno, a convict who was Jim's cellmate.

Jim said that Bruno was a junkie, a tough, bully addict. Arrested and put in jail, Bruno beat up anyone brought into his cellblock, just to prove his toughness. Then Jim was put into the cell with Bruno, but Bruno took a liking to Jim and didn't offer to fight him. Jim witnessed to Bruno about Christ, but then Jim was bailed out. Later, when Jim was returned to prison, there was Bruno.

But now Bruno had his shaggy locks trimmed neatly and had a clean look about him. Jim asked Bruno what had happened to him. Bruno replied, "I'm a Christian now, man. One day as I sat here in my cell I got to reading some literature and I gave my heart over to God. And now I'm a Christian." Jim told us that the fellows Bruno used to beat up now turned the tables. They mocked him and threw his clothes out of the bullpen.

Jim said he became so disgusted one afternoon that he yelled, "Come on, Bruno, let's go in there and tear those guys up!"

Bruno replied, "No, that's not the right way to do it." Jim was shocked, but followed Bruno's advice. Later, Bruno, who faced a possible ten-year sentence, said to cellblock mates, "I'm not going to jail. I'm walking out."

When Bruno went to court, he had no time to consult his attorney nor to notify his parents. Alone, he faced the court and was given a sentence of five years in Raiford Prison in Florida. When he came back to the cellblock, he was whistling. Everyone thought he had been freed, but he said "Man, got myself five years, but I'm not doing it. I'm not doing any time."

His cellmates began to jeer and ridicule him. They sneered, "Where is your God now, man? How religious are you?" Bruno was sent to a central Florida disbursing point. There he contacted his attorney, who had him brought back to West Palm Beach for a new court hearing. Because he had been sentenced without benefit of counsel, Bruno was released and returned to his home. Jim told us that he had received a letter from Bruno, written from Bruno's home.

Jim said, "God opened the doors for Bruno after the court closed them tight. The court did the same to me and God let me out. He doesn't want me to go back on the streets again." We asked him why he didn't yield himself to God's will. He shrugged his shoulders, saying, "I don't know. I want to but I can't do it."

At church one Sunday I noticed that Jim was missing. I had a hunch he had run away and, after checking with some of the other residents, learned he had done just that. He apparently had planned his departure for some time. I had felt he would do it, but didn't know when. Now it had happened.

That afternoon I received a telephone call from Jim. He apologized for running away and said he wanted to come back. I told him, "Jim, you can't be pulling this kind of thing. By rights I was supposed to notify the authorities as soon as I learned you were gone." He asked if I had done so, and I told him no. I added that if he wanted to come back, he first would need to talk with Glenn Bondurant. I directed him to the Covenant Presbyterian Church where Glenn was to speak that night.

When Glenn returned to the halfway house, Jim was with him. He claimed to have rededicated his life to the Lord—but I later learned he was biding his time. For on the following Thursday Jim ran away, this time for good. A month went by before he called me. He told me he was "messed up." He said, "I haven't touched drugs. I haven't even smoked a reefer. But I'm just messed up. What should I do?"

I urged him to give himself up, to call the probation-parole office and tell them just what he was experiencing. I told him he might well have a slight mental disorder, and that he should seek help. He promised to turn himself in. I turned away from the telephone, feeling completely crushed. Jim needed all the help he could get, and we were eager to do what we could, but he seemed unwilling, or unable, to let us help.

Glenn and I often pray for Jim—and the thousands of Jims like him—who struggle by themselves to do what God alone can do. We pray that instead of turning farther away from God, they will see his open arms of love and power, that they will let him be their strength and save them from sin.

11

Turn the Whole World On!

When Jim left our program, I knew that Judge Mac-
Intosh would be soured on letting other addicts come to
Turning Point. Still, I felt an obligation to let the court
know what had happened. As the author of the book,
Tough Love, expressed it, you have to be tough, yet love
those who have transgressed. So I notified the probation-
parole office, then personally called Judge MacIntosh to
relate the details of Jim's leaving.

The judge thanked me for calling him and expressed
his own disappointment over Jim's dropping out of our
program. Later we learned that Jim wrote a revealing
letter to both the probation officer and to the judge. It
read in part:

> I don't know if you will remember me, but I am
> the boy Vince Guerra and you went to the trouble
> of getting a mitigation of sentence for, so I could
> go to Turning Point. By now I guess you know I
> have left. I want you to know that it wasn't the pro-
> gram that I left. It is one of the best there is. The
> staff there really takes an interest in the guys. I hope
> my action won't hinder anyone else from Palm
> Beach County who wants help.
>
> I have always been running: if I'm not going into
> jail, I'm coming out. I am clean from drugs (thanks

to Vince and Glenn), but am unhappy because they were counting on me and I let them and everybody down. I know it's time to take on my responsibilities to my fellowman and God, and I know running is not the way.

I was going to talk to my probation officer, but I chickened out because all I could think of was, back to jail I go again. I am sorry for all the trouble I have caused everyone. I hope more guys get a chance at Turning Point, with no regard to my actions.

Jim

We could only pray that Jim's letter might have some good effect upon the court in future cases where defendants indicated willingness to come into our program.

But regardless of that matter, things are far from quiet at Turning Point Halfway House. Because Barbara Bondurant had to go to Jacksonville, Florida, for a few days, we persuaded Glenn to go with her. His work had kept him tied down more than was good for a person. Just before the excited couple left, Glenn and I were in my office discussing operational matters. I kidded Glenn about his not forgetting to come back to work, then he walked out.

Standing in the hall, waiting for Glenn to leave, was Bob Dolan. He indicated he wished to talk with me alone. We stepped into my office and Bob blurted out, "Vince, I'd like to make a commitment to Christ. I mean, I did at Virginia Schmitt's last night." Mrs. Schmitt is a remarkable lay worker in the fast-growing Coral Ridge Presbyterian Church. She has a Bible study in her home on Monday and Tuesday nights, the Tuesday night attendance averaging between one hundred and two hundred youths and young adults.

119

Bob, by proving himself trustworthy, had earned the privilege of going to Mrs. Schmitt's home on Tuesday nights. While there, he had accepted Christ as his Savior silently, with no one counseling him. Now he wanted assurance that his commitment was valid, that his faith and experience were genuine. He wanted to share his new-found faith with someone, and he had come to me. He asked me to pray with him.

After we prayed, I advised Bob to begin reading the four Gospels, beginning with John. Then I confessed to Bob that, because of his former religious background, I had almost despaired of his ever accepting Christ. Since that had been my own background, I knew the difficulties involved. But Bob really turned on to Christ that night. His life had been filled with problems, and he knew it. And he knew that the road ahead would not be easy.

I thought Glenn had already departed from Jacksonville, but just then he came walking into my office, so I told him about Bob's new faith in Christ. We rejoiced together, and I knew Glenn was especially happy, because he had spent many hours counseling with Bob. Now Bob really had something to sing about as a member of the choir in the church he attends.

The following day a young black man named Fred Green came into our program. A well-built fellow, Fred had been on heroin for seven years, destroying his marriage and wrecking his life. He was unable to see his four children, kept in custody by his separated wife. Fred was really strung out. Gradually we learned about his drug use.

Fred started using drugs while working as a hospital aide. There some college-age sophisticates turned him on.

He liked his first encounter with drugs, and within a short time he was hooked—an addict. Fred told me about the times he stole demerol from the hospital. He said that when a patient was made ready for surgery, a shot of demerol was given for sedation. Often, the half-empty drug bottle was left on a shelf. Fred took the little vials, collected the demerol in them, and spent the nights in drug-induced euphoria.

One night, however, he was just ready to take a half-empty bottle of what he first thought was demerol—but which he later identified as a highly dangerous type of procaine. As he picked up the vial, he thought he heard someone call his name. Hurriedly he moved away from the drug. "Who called my name?" he asked his co-worker.

"I didn't call you," came the reply.

Bewildered, Fred was afraid to go back to the drug vial because his co-worker watched him too closely. That night when he arrived home, Fred turned on the television to watch the news. He heard the shocking story of a girl who had died from an overdose of procaine, the very drug he had been about to take from the hospital! The reporter said the drug was fatal within minutes after injection into a vein—the very method Fred intended to use. Realizing how fortunate he had been, Fred threw himself down on the couch and began to cry. He knew he needed help. The next day he came to Turning Point.

In order to find out where his head was at—determine his emotional balance—I asked him what he thought of our program, how he liked our classes, the food, lodging. Having been in a couple of other programs, Fred said he felt ours was about the best place he'd ever been in. I asked him what he thought of committing his life to

Jesus Christ. He replied, "Man, if I'm going to break away from dope and all that goes with it, He's the only one who'll be able to pull me out."

Fred expressed genuine concern about his family. He wanted to return to his wife and children. I walked over to him and asked if he was earnest enough to kneel and pray. He said he was, so we knelt there in my office. I said, "If you're really sincere about accepting Jesus Christ, ask him to come into your heart and take away the desire for dope."

I put my arm around his shoulders and together we prayed. Fred asked Jesus Christ to come into his heart. Then he looked at me and said, "Man, I feel great!"

From the reality of my own experience I replied, "Fred, it's only the beginning. Christ will really give you a whole new concept, a whole new life, as you look to him for direction." It really does me good to see an addict come into the Turning Point program and allow his life to be made over completely new by the power of Jesus Christ.

Yet, some of the most pathetic cases of addiction are those who have been made so not of their own will. Such was the case with Tom. Tom called our office one day, saying he was a veteran back from Vietnam. He had stepped on a land mine, which had blown off part of one leg. The large muscle in the calf of his leg was shattered, part of it missing. Tom had lost his identity as an able-bodied man, and was emotionally strung out. His whole life seemed to be crashing about him.

His story was that while in the hospital, he had become dependent upon morphine, but upon release had been completely cut off. Feeling the need for drug-induced relief, he finally turned to heroin, and was quickly hooked.

He had been on heroin for three years at the time he came to us.

Tom felt part of his problem was his inability to walk normally. Through our Turning Point ministry contacts, we were able to have Tom examined by a Dr. George, a surgeon who specializes in bone surgery. Dr. George explained to Tom and me that he would untie the muscles in Tom's leg and re-tie them so Tom could walk with scarcely a limp. He was eager to have the operation, but first he had to be de-toxified to get the craving for drugs out of his system.

The thirteen days Tom spent at the Coral Ridge Psychiatric Hospital were highly successful. He was dried out and ready to enter a medical hospital for surgery on his crippled leg. Dr. George performed a masterful job on Tom, who was able to move his foot and leg much better following surgery and therapy. We at Turning Point praised God for his concern and care for Tom.

Tom responded well to the medication given him and seemed to have no desire for drugs. He expected to be released within two weeks, and we looked forward to having him in our program. Then one day Tom signed himself out of the hospital and was gone. No one knows where he went. His mother has not heard from him. We have had no word about him or from him. It seems so strange that he would accept our help and then leave without a single word of explanation. Yet, that often happens in a ministry of faith, and we only trust that something we have said or done will remind that person of God's love and mercy.

Steve was another veteran of the Vietnam conflict. He was mixed up emotionally. He had started smoking marijuana while in "Nam," as he called it. When his kneecap was blown off, he was given morphine to deaden the pain, both while on the battlefield and in the hospital. Then he learned that his wife had been unfaithful while he was overseas. Discharged from the paratroopers, Steve went home a bitter, crippled, defeated man. He soon became the town drunk.

A pastor from Steve's hometown in Michigan called us to see if we might be able to help Steve. He described Steve's condition and, against our usual policy of seeing an individual first, we accepted Steve on the condition that he would really seek help for his total need. He came to us, a mixed-up, confused, young man.

We learned in a hurry that Steve had no love for church people. He thought most Christians sat on their best intentions all week, that they were stuffy, caring nothing at all about the problems of young people. While anti-church, Steve loved the Bible and said he loved Jesus Christ, His problem was deeply emotional, attributed in part to poor education, his past family life, and his wife's unfaithfulness.

A letter Steve wrote to his mother while he was with us indicates something about his difficulty:

> Mom, I love you and care about you very, very much. To me, you are the best mom. I will always care. I cannot understand why life has been so hard on you. God knows that if I could, I would do anything for your happiness. I'd make the world a part-time place for you and stomp the teeth in of all the people who ever hurt you. Jesus will make everything even, I'm sure.
>
> I love you. Please do not let me down, mom. Love Jesus. Stop drinking, go get help. Pray, mom. Pray

for a change of life. Accept Jesus. I STILL CARE. Mom, God's will be done with Jesus' help always. I'm going to live for him. Jesus saves. God's Word is true.

Mom, he saved me a lot of times: when I was born, in a car I was driving, in Vietnam, in Dominican Republic, in everyday life. He saved me from myself, from all my troubles, from my very thinking. I apologize from my heart for all your troubles. I cannot help you, only Jesus can. He alone. I have enough troubles in my life. I cannot carry your burdens. Call on Jesus. He can.

If you will, please send my check to me if it came to the house. Then I will have money for Christmas. I put the ketchup on my chest to see if you would care. You said you did not. Then I wiped it off and told the cops you called that there was not anything wrong, because you went and got drunk. Mom, I love you. Quit killing yourself! It's not worth it at all. I know that I almost did on drugs and hate. Change your heart. Ask Jesus for help. Change your life is also part of it, too. All my love, all my prayers. Your number one son,

Steve, and you know me.
P.S. Mom, I'm A-O.K. Don't worry. I'm with people who love me. Most of all they love Jesus. Card will follow in a week or so.

Steve's mind was messed up because he had sniffed glue, lacquer thinner, gasoline, benzine, and other solvents. He could not retain much of what he read or heard, and only with effort worked on the level of a seventh-grade student. I sympathized with him, because I remembered what it was like to be a slow, inefficient reader.

Both Glenn and I worked diligently with Steve, counseling him in spiritual concerns. He tended to become moody at times, and caused trouble among our residents by picking on persons. Then came the day when Steve accepted Christ as his Lord and Savior. What a change we noted then. His attitude became several-hundred percent better. He grew spiritually at a rapid pace, then in about four months he wanted to return home.

Although we preferred that he stay with us longer, we knew he had a burden for his mother and his community, so we bade him Godspeed and he returned to Michigan. We pray that his witness will bless others who need Christ, and that Steve will remain strong. Many young men and women are being turned on to Jesus Christ through the ministry of Turning Point. The coffee houses are reaching many turned off youths, and helping them to have something worth living for. We are eager to get the message of Christ to thousands of young persons. Whether a youth is in crime or merely having trouble understanding his parents, we seek opportunities to be of service in Christian love.

Currently Glenn Bondurant, co-director of Turning Point, is preparing high school curriculum so we can have our own school program at Turning Point Halfway House. We also hope to offer a two-year junior college program in the future. Rehabilitation without adequate training in academic skills is futile, we believe. We seek to provide practical tools to enable former addicts to obtain responsible positions in trades and industry.

Increasingly, my time is spent in fulfilling speaking engagements in many parts of the United States. Barbara Bondurant often speaks to women's groups, and I speak for youth meetings, retreats, and crusades. Results from these encounters with young persons are simply amazing. It really thrills me to be able to present the gospel story to hundreds of young persons and then watch the response as one after another yield themselves to the abundant life Christ offers.

Then there are side effects, too. Recently, while on my way to Springfield, Ohio, I met an Air Force major. Falling into conversation, I quickly detected his sensitivity to spiritual things and asked him if he were a Christian. He replied that ten years before, he had committed his life to Christ during a meeting at which Dr. Elton Trueblood spoke. He confessed that he had not kept that commitment. But he was quite willing, even eager, to bow his head and offer himself again in surrender to the Lord.

On February 15, 1971, I flew toward home after an exciting trip to northern states where I had some wonderfully refreshing meetings. I was spiritually elated as the huge jet plane I was riding settled down on the runway at Fort Lauderdale airport. I looked forward to meeting my wife, Ruth, and our growing son, Jackie. But though I looked and looked, Ruth was nowhere in sight. This wasn't like her, I knew. Could something be wrong? I wondered.

Then I caught sight of Sue Mulheim, one of our staff workers at Turning Point. Breathlessly she told me she had brought Ruth to me, but that Ruth decided she had better hurry to the hospital before our second child made its arrival at the airport.

Throwing my luggage into Sue's car, we sped off to the hospital. There, not much later, our beautiful daughter, Jeanine Marie, was born—all nine pounds four ounces of her!

So now I have one more reason why I want to get the whole world hooked—on God!